# Daddy Survival Guide

## By Alex Willis

Visit www.justfordaddy.com
For Daddy Tricks and Tips, fun games and downloadable
coloring books (and man stuff of course)

www.justfordaddy.com is an imprint of DB Publishing
For more information about permission, email
info@dbpublishinghouse.com

2$^{nd}$ Edition, Copyright 2009 by Alex Willis
www.DBPublishinghouse.com & www.justfordaddy.com

ISBN:  978-0-9819525-1-2

A personal note from the author:

This is a guide for men. It is worthless material for the eyes of the 'gentler' of the species. They have their books, all girly and full of advice from their kindred sisters. (Yawn)… sorry, we men need our own book. One that highlights only the important things to know, the things they tend to overlook at birthing classes and the things our mothers just figured wasn't important for us to know. These are things we wish our fathers told us had they been more involved in the process.

If you picked up this guide you must first understand the layout:

> ➢ This book was written to be to the point, no fluff-n-stuff
> ➢ This book is intended to be entertaining because books on this subject are boring! No, seriously, they are filled with good information and wonderful for someone to know…but very boring!
> ➢ This book does contain adult material, let's face it, if you got her pregnant, you were doing adult things so suck it up and deal with the manliness of this book
> ➢ This book has segments of completely unrelated topics to keep it interesting, after all, how much baby studying can you really be expected to do.
> ➢ This book is broken down into 3 sections:
>   - The Never Ending, Hormone Filled, Fear and Stress Increasing 9 months of Pregnancy
>   - The Pain of Labor and Delivery, for her too
>   - The confusing first few weeks of the baby you can't believe they let you go home with considering you have no formal training and you are an OJT parent
> ➢ This book is considerate of all lifestyles and never assumes the relationship of a man and a woman, just that they are parents of a child. So if you want to make babies with a complete stranger, it's really none of my business…just be a great dad!

- ➢ Last, take this book for what it is. Real world advice from one dad to another. Sure, I am a great dad and have been one many times over for many years and if you are lucky you might actually pick up some helpful tips to not botch up the whole daddy experience.
- ➢ And lastly, never believe that last means that it is the last word spoken. This story only begins and ends when you die. If you haven't figured it out by this point, you will be a dad forever!
- ➢ Good Luck!

If you enjoy this book, keep it. Don't pass it on. Tell other dads to buy their own. Next thing you know they will want to borrow your car or your boat and bring it back with vomit on the floor. Not cool. Keep in mind that there are elements that are important for you to keep from your woman. The notes contained in these hallowed pages are designed to make you look smart. If she knows you get all your insight from a book, what do you think that makes you look like? Seriously, you need this book more than I thought! Perhaps you should buy an extra copy as you will likely misplace this one and you can't really ask her where you put it.


Alex Willis


> This book is dedicated to my very patient wife who didn't hold me accountable when I didn't do everything I advise other men to do. Although, she does hold me to a higher standard... Thanks Jennifer.

# Table of Contents

**Part II – "It's time, what?  What do you mean??  OMG!.. Where's my keys, the bag, did you remember that thing you knew I'd forget? How do we get to the hospital?  WTF, I need to call my mom…." – Thiese are very important chapters about the time you've been ~~dreading~~ looking forward to**

**Part III – Life's little instruction book for a dad with no clue on what to do with a baby.., someone at the hospital should have stopped you at the door and made you take a practical exam before allowing you to go home**

# Part I – She's knocked up, now what?

## Chapter 1 – Getting prepared for what's expected

First and foremost, you need to understand that you and your baby mama are **both** pregnant.  It is a simple truth that men don't feel the same way as women do about being pregnant.  It is impossible to understand what it is like having something living and growing inside of you, it is also impossible to understand the hormonal changes.  While some professionals will tell you to empathize with your significant other, just accept that you cannot understand in theory what it means to be pregnant and just tell her that you are 'both' pregnant.  Sometimes all they want to hear are the words.  To them it means that you are as committed as she is to the pregnancy.

She will likely start picking up books on pregnancy or subscribing to websites that will track her pregnancy.  She will also start looking for a doctor to monitor the pregnancy and decide where the delivery will happen.  If you want to be a hero... scratch that... a superhero, do it for her.  Go out and pick up *What to Expect When You're Expecting* and *A Girlfriends Guide to Pregnancy*, also pick up a pregnancy planning guide with pages to fill in important dates (if you are a man of steel you will find the expected delivery date and circle it before giving her the guide).  She will use it to record feelings about the pregnancy, gifts, visitors, possible baby names and on and on.  Think of it like when you were in Junior High and girls all carried notebooks with Unicorns on the cover and they wrote all kinds of things in them about boys they liked, girls they hated and whatever else the mysteries are of pre-teen female.

Another action that will put you more in touch with the pregnancy is to contact your insurance company and help identify OB/GYN specialists in the area and make some preliminary calls.  **DO NOT** schedule the appointment.  Ultimately it is her choice whom she will see and as it is her body, she will want to carefully select the professional that she will want to check her out 'down there'.  But she will appreciate you helping with the preliminary search.  Make sure you understand the difference between an OB, GYN, ARNP and MidWife

> OB is the abbreviation for an Obstetrician who is a physician that has successfully completed specialized education and training in the management of pregnancy, labor, and pueperium (the time-period directly following childbirth).

> GYN is a physician who has studied Gynecology which deals with the female reproductive system

You will almost always find that doctors who are working with the pregnancy are identified as both and seen as OB/GYN.  When a woman is not pregnant, she may see her family physician unless it has to do with female issues and it is at that time that she would likely see a Gynecologist.

ARNP or Advanced Registered Nurse Practitioner is a very experienced and educated nurse that in some cases functions like a doctor. These nurses are often seen in OB/GYN offices as the primary caregiver for both consultation and delivery. They are normally under the direction of an OB/GYN physician and consulted on cases.

Midwife is an old world description of a woman who aids in the delivery of babies. They were typically wise about conditions and situations that could cause the delivery to be difficult or would require alternative methods to push the baby out. Most midwives in the US are ARNP educated and specialize in the midwifery. They are highly educated nurses, to the level of a physician and choose to just deliver babies. It is becoming more common for hospitals to use midwifes instead of OB/GYN doctors as they are cheaper and there are simply more available than OB/GYN doctors. The patient benefits by not having an overworked physician do the procedure, and working with someone whose only focus is delivering babies.

Remember to let her choose who will deliver and who she feels comfortable seeing. It is kind of like you trying to decide which doctor is going to do a proctologic or prostate exam... and not just eyeing him up to see if he is gay or has big hands.

**Make appointments to suit both your schedules**

Doctor appointments will come slow in the beginning and as the delivery date gets closer they will go from monthly visits to biweekly to weekly. You must remember that this is scary for her and she needs the support no matter how much she may try to convince you otherwise. It may not be possible to make all appointments if you have a normal work schedule as doctors' offices typically have normal work schedules as well. In your selection process for a doctor/midwife, you may want to find out about evening hours and satellite locations that could be closer to your home or work.

There are a handful of key appointments you do not want to miss (and she would not forgive you if you did). Those include the first appointment where it is "officially" confirmed that she is knocked up. She will **want you** to be **excited** with her, and even though she may have taken a dozen at home pregnancy tests, it is **"not the same"** as a medical professional stating, "ma'am, our tests indicate a positive, meaning you are pregnant". A special note here, whether you take a home pregnancy test or go to the doctor where she will pee in a cup, the test is always attempting to indicate a hormone called b-hCG (Beta Human Chroionic Gondotropin Hormone). If you want to impress her and her friends, you can whip out the hormone hCG as the indicator, but you also need to understand what it does. It's like the invisibility cloak of a famous little boy wizard, where the body is fooled into believing that there isn't an invading growth that should be destroyed. Understand also that this particular hormone that is masking the baby from the body triggers other hormones that may also have adverse affects on the mother, such as mood swings. (More than normal if that's possible).

Other critical appointments may include genetic screening where a number of questions are asked about families, medical histories and the like. Any visit to the doctor is a good time to ask questions.

**RULE #1** - There are no stupid questions. This statement may be cliché but true, and as a father you are expected to be ignorant about women's issues and pregnancy. So if you want to know if you can have sex while she is in her first, second and third trimester... ask!  If you want to sound intelligent, ask questions about gestational diabetes a precursor to preeclampsia[1] which could impact her during the pregnancy.  This is the body's inability to process sugar much like a diabetic; however it only occurs during the pregnancy.  It can be identified by measuring proteins in urine which is why she needs to pee in a cup at every visit.  There are other tests that may measure more accurately if this dangerous condition exists.  It is very important to learn more about this subject and be prepared if it occurs to her.

The ultrasound appointment is a big and important time for her as it is the first time you and she will see baby and very likely the first time the heartbeat will be heard clearly.  For most women, seeing it makes it more real.  For most men, seeing the skeletal image on the screen swimming in amniotic fluid causes your own mind to start swimming, things like, 'How am I going to afford this'... 'What if I don't know what to do when the baby comes'... 'How do I ensure it's a boy and that he grows up to be a professional football player'... you know, the normal stuff.  Just remember to make this appointment one of your top priorities, you will find it an experience worth noting.

Make sure you schedule time off near the due date (the day she is supposed to give birth, they always assume you know what due date means).  Inform your employer that you need some flexibility as the baby will not likely come according to schedule.  Make sure that family members who are planning on helping during that time do the same.  When she does go into labor, one of the first phone calls you need to make is to your employer to confirm that

---

[1] Pregnancy-induced hypertension (PIH), which is also called toxemia or preeclampsia (say "pre-ee-clamp-see-ah"), is a problem that occurs in some women during pregnancy. It can happen during the second half of pregnancy. Your doctor will look for the following signs of PIH: high blood pressure, swelling that doesn't go away and large amounts of protein in your urine.

she is in labor.  Do not call until the doctor sees her and identifies that it is actually labor.  Women will have false labor near the end of the pregnancy called Braxton-Hicks contractions and you may make several practice runs to the hospital.

**1960 Austin Healey BT7**

**SURVIVAL TIP**

Normal TIP: It's a good idea to go out and buy her a gift when you find out she's pregnant! You may also want to consider buying something for the baby too. Some ideas include:

- A cool maternity top (make sure you know her size, but typically S, M, L, XL will do)
- A spa treatment or day at a salon (It will make her feel better about her body changing and help relax some of those hormonal swings)
- A silver plated rattle (this can be inscribed later after the baby is born)
- A sleeper, blanket or bear
- A charm bracelet with a new charm for each month that she is pregnant (this is a great way to pass the months and keeping track of progress)


**Surviving Pregnancy TIP: Pregnancy & Water**

As she continues through her pregnancy, it is critical that she drink a lot of water. Eight - 8 oz glasses at least. This will help with the blood needed to support the new life developing in her. It will also keep her own fluids moving and reduce swelling and blood pressure. This does not replace the requirement for milk which will keep her body from losing calcium that the baby is taking from her to develop its bones. The first sign of calcium deficiency is weakened teeth and cavities. She may feel bloated from drinking so much, but by listening to her own body she will know what and when to drink.  It's your job to keep on her.

**Survival TIP:  How to distill water in the wild**

You can create a solar still in the event of emergency.  You will need a large plastic sheet or tarp to make a solar still. Dig a conical hole about four-feet wide at the top and coming to a point about two-feet deep. The bottom of the hole should be in the very center (equal distance from all sides). The slope of the sides isn't critical. Put a medium size pot at the very bottom of the hole. Then lay your plastic sheet over the top of the hole and put a medium size rock (about one-pound) in the center of the sheet just above the pot which will be directly underneath the sheet. Put heavy rocks on top of your plastic sheet all around the outside of the hole to keep the sheet from touching the inner sloping sides of the hole. The center of the sheet should be about 18 inches below the surface of the ground but about 6 inches above the pot. Wait 24 hours. Water vapor will form on the underside of your tarp and drain down to its lowest point (beneath your one-pound rock) and then drip into your pot in the bottom of the hole. On hot days and cold nights you can collect about one-pint of water per 24-hour period.

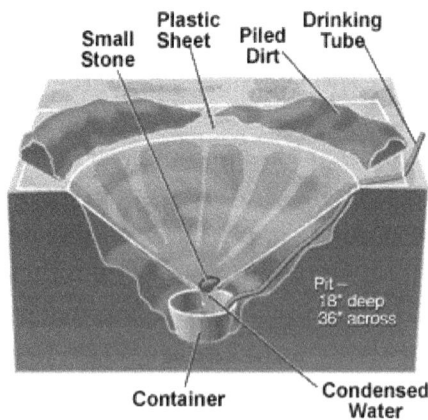

Small Stone · Plastic Sheet · Piled Dirt · Drinking Tube · Pit – 18" deep 36" across · Container · Condensed Water

## Chapter 2 – The T&A is Kicking and other Physical Changes

She will get bigger, in her belly as well as other parts of her body. If this is her first pregnancy, most likely her hips will get bigger as well.  This is due to her body needing to make room for a baby to fit through her hips and out the birthing canal and the bones and cartilage will not move back to what they were before the pregnancy.  Most men enjoy some of the new curves which include enlarged breasts.  Unfortunately the breasts return to a smaller size after delivery, however if she chooses to breast feed they will maintain a larger size as long as she is extracting milk.  If you like the new look, realize that it comes with leakage which baby likes but men normally don't.  Also, while you may find some of these changes enticing and inviting, she may feel completely different.  Her body is changing and things no longer fit so her esteem is likely dropping.  It is your job to remind her how beautiful she really is and that her baby changes don't change anything.

Most men take full advantage of these changes to do some of their own.  They will often have an extra serving at dinner, or ask for more ice cream for dessert.  We like to call it empathizing with the growth of the mommy, but the truth is that as it seems she is letting herself go, it should be okay to let ourselves go.  The only problem is that she will loose a great amount of girth once the baby is delivered.  We men won't.

As described earlier, she will undergo some mood changes. Sometimes these are extreme and sometimes they are mild.  She may laugh one minute and cry the next.  She may feel stable and then insecure.  She will love and hate you at the same time.

While we know it is the hormones that are causing this problem, it's like telling your drunk buddy that he's had way too much to drink. In other words, complete denial. The best thing to do is to be prepared to wait out the bad moods, be whatever she needs until it passes. If she wants to cry, give her a tissue and tell her you understand. If she is mad, find a chore and go do it. If she wants sex...well, do whatever she needs you to do.

Hormones may also cause her body to desire specific food. The body as a machine is constantly feeding information about what it required to keep all systems in check. It gets confused because of the hormones and the woman believes that only a Peanut Butter and Jelly and Pickle sandwich will do. Some will tell you that the woman's pregnant body is identifying a lack of a vitamin or mineral and it is seeking it through known flavors and that it recognizes the taste to the mineral. So in the PB&J with Pickle, it is likely that she is low on zinc. I don't have a habit of sucking on zinc, but the salty, sour metallic taste of the pickle would imply a mineral, the PB&J (strawberry) identify a certain earthy flavor which could make us conclude zinc. There is no real scientific study if this is true or not other then the fact that women get cravings. It's a fun game to play with her as to what and why her body is asking for pickled herring and orange sherbet.

The baby's mommy may also experience morning sickness in the first trimester of her pregnancy. (Note: Morning sickness is loose term in that it is not restricted to the mornings). She may feel nauseous and want to throw up. The best cure is saltines or a clear soda. If you are up to it, pretend like you're still dating and you've been partying late and you need to hold her hair back to keep the mess focused. While this last bit is a joke, be aware that she will likely want to be alone during the morning sickness times. It will likely pass after the first trimester when the hormone levels normalize.

Trimester – Pregnancy occurs over a 9 month period and is broken into three equal parts called trimesters. The first 3 months of pregnancy is known as the first trimester and other than morning sickness not much is visibly different.

During the first and second trimesters a woman will generate 40% more blood than normal. The plain and simple explanation is that she needs more blood for the baby. This may cause her to bloat, swell and have high blood pressure. Her heart rate will also increase during this time. While these things are not new or unusual, they should be monitored carefully. There may be many times when she needs to sit with her feet up to alleviate some of the swelling that is occurring. DO NOT rub the bottom of the feet to try and remove some of the pressure. Some experts will tell you that certain touch points can induce labor.

Gas... while it's not a pretty subject its very real. She may feel more gassy than ever and may have some reeking, worthy of a man, gas. This is normal and it passes, just pretend that it's Monday night and your are watching the game with some of your best buds and burping and farting are the norm. She is there in full swing!

Pain... She will experience all kinds of aches and pains through the pregnancy. Some of the worst and scariest are the round tendons that hold the uterus in place. They are accustomed to holding a small vessel and not doing much work. All of a sudden the small space is growing large and they are being pulled taut and the pain can feel like cramps. The woman may fear a miscarriage and worry that something is not right. Don't worry, everything is okay and should simply be remarked at the next doctors visit who will also reassure her. Don't be offended if she doesn't believe you, it is the nature of women to disbelieve anything the person who put her in that condition says. If she does continue to feel cramps or shows signs of bleeding, definitely stop reading this book and call a doctor! These are signs of more significant problems.

Other pain could come from the breasts that are growing at an astronomical rate only to be rivaled with the baby bump. That growth comes with its own pain due to changes in glands and weight. The breasts will likely be sensitive in the first trimester and continue to feel uncomfortable throughout the pregnancy. The change in size to the breasts, uterus and hips will also cause aches and pains that are typically felt in the lower back. Get used to rubbing, long and hard...just like you'd like it!

Sinus pressure, mucus build up and allergies are not unheard of during a pregnancy. Some old wives will tell you that women become super-sensitive to the extraneous world. Anthropologists who may argue that we have inert instincts, believe that our ancient ancestors needed to be cautious of predators or poisonous vegetation and adopted this extra heightened sensory perception. Still, scientists today say that the body is simply reacting to changes in the body's chemistry. Whatever the reason, some women will experience an abundance of snot. There I said it, call it mucus if you like, there is just a lot more of it than normal. This may lead to sinus pressure and headaches, and in some cases bring on certain seasonal allergies.

**TIP: One of the things on the shower gift list will be a diaper bag. This is a huge necessity and should not be overlooked. When carting a baby around you need a place to store all kinds of things...bottles, diapers, wipes, a clothespin for your nose. Make sure that you identify a man bag for the rare times you must take the baby on your own! There is nothing worse than going to the mall with your son carrying a Pink Flower diaper bag over**

your shoulder and seeing the local high school football coach and stopping him to talk about your boys throwing arm...

Consider purchasing a Daddy Survival Kit...I included everything a man needs to tend to his baby. Go to our website, www.justfordaddy.com

## Chapter 3 – Taking care of Business, and other things she would like if we did

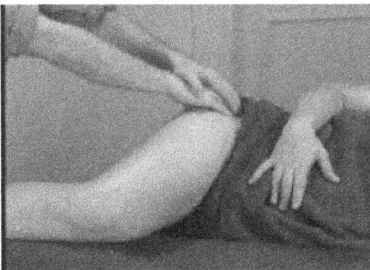

Although it's a foreign concept for most of us men, massage is not just a channel to get sex. And while we simply can't help but to touch a woman and believe that it's going to lead somewhere, we as men need to become a little more enlightened and understand that it is truly all about her. Of course, if she feels like she wants to afterward... what they hey, we're guys right.

A massage not only helps reduce pain, but it aids the woman throughout her pregnancy and has some very nice additional benefits. She will definitely owe you big time for the following:

1. Elimination of waste through the lymphatic and circulatory systems. If you are a man, you are certainly asking yourself if we are talking about poo here, and if so, count me out. The answer is yes and no. The body moves fluid and blood through these systems to help feed our bodies. Our intestines provide the nutrients to feed our bodies. What isn't used up in the intestines eventually becomes poo. The waste however that we are talking about is the fluids that are moving slowly and becoming old or unclean. Think about your engine shortly after an oil change. Clean oil lubricates the moving parts and it runs like butter. Massage will help push out the old fluids to allow for fresh fluids to grease up those moving parts. As a result, she would enjoy an energy burst.

2. Blood Pressure management is important during pregnancy. By massaging and getting the fluids inside the body moving, it reduces the amount of work the heart needs to do thus minimizing varicosities and keeping the pressure under control.

3. Muscle pain, cramping, tightening, stiffness and tension or knots are typical during pregnancy. Increased circulation during a massage can reduce some of the pressure on weight bearing joints in turn relieving some of the problem pain areas.

4. Hormones, hormones, hormones. In general, women are just moody. You get them pregnant and it's like taking a

magnifying glass to an ant hill. It has been proven that massage can reduce stress hormone levels which can relieve depression or anxiety often intensified by confronting new expectations and fears about parenting.

5.  Mucus membranes can become inflamed during pregnancy resulting in sinus pressure and headaches. Specific acupressure points on the face and nose can provide significant relief.

6.  Swelling especially in the feet and ankles are common as pregnant women tend to retain an excess of water. Massage helps these fluids move and absorb into the systems than can help evacuate the water. Avoid rubbing the bottom of the feet, and not just because they are disgusting. If the bottom of the feet swells, the best approach to relieve the pain is to walk. The pressure created from walking will help push fluids better than any massage.

7.  Baby is hungry and lives on the blood and nutrients fed through the umbilical cord. By improving blood circulation, fresh oxygen and nutrients are pumped into the baby providing for better nourishment.

8.  "Relax and be flexible", says the hormones to the body. During pregnancy, hormones are working to relax the tendons and ligaments to accommodate a growing baby belly. Still, there is some discomfort to the muscles that can be relieved by a massage. By relaxing the muscles there could be a decrease in muscular cramps and increased flexibility which can facilitate in the birthing process.

9. A knock out drug... let's face it, after a good massage (like good sex), all our body wants to do is sleep. Again, we are guys and our minds will always steer to the latter, but please stay with my analogy here. Most women will experience sleeplessness during their pregnancy and will become weary. If you can get her completely relaxed through massage, she could sleep much better and will thank you in the morning.

10. Labor might not seem to be the appropriate time for a massage, and by now your hands are sure to be tired from months of your own labor. However, this is an ideal time to do a little massage, which if appropriately applied can help reduce lower back and labor pain. Many midwives use massage techniques to help ease the delivery, but that doesn't mean you can shirk your responsibility. Remember one of your previous survival tips, as she is cussing you out and promising to rip off certain areas of your anatomy, focus on rubbing massage lotion on one of those Hawaiian Topic bikini girls and... bliss. (By the way, it may be a good idea to not let her read this book, if she found out what you were focusing on she may carry out her previous threat!

**PETS:** If you thought your honey do list was long enough before, now that she's pregnant it will get longer. If you have cats that use a litter box, it is now all on you to clean it out. This is because cats' fecal matter carries a nasty little bug that could cause a miscarriage. This holds true for

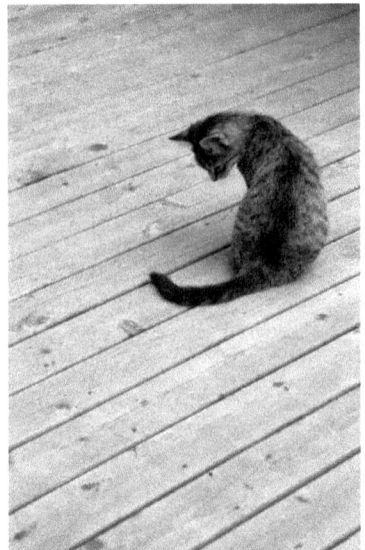

gardening as well, for it is nearly impossible to tell if a cat has used the flower beds as their litter box.  It is just safe and sane to keep her out.  There is nothing wrong with petting and feeding the cat... it's just the messy stuff that she needs to avoid.

And since we are on the subject of chores, due to simple physical limitations you will find that more things will be on your plate. Heavy things which were already your job get to stay your job!

Time to show off your manliness!  That includes carrying groceries in the house, putting objects up on higher shelves (her equilibrium will play heck with her body and her balance is always in question), carrying things up and down stairs, opening and closing blinds and windows.  A simple rule, if it's heavy or requires her to stretch, it is your job.  Other non-traditional jobs for men that at some point in the pregnancy will become manly include washing dishes and cooking.  There is a point when her belly won't allow her to reach the dishes in the sink or bend over to put them in the dishwasher.  Also, stop to think about the proximity of the baby to the stove.  Of course the baby will be well insulated, but the mommy won't be and would be a very unhappy camper if she got a belly burn.

This is not the time to take up bungee jumping or extreme mountain biking.  However, it *is* a good time to start a regular walking regimen if you don't already have an exercise routine.  As the months go by it will be more difficult for her to get around and the better shape that she is in going into and during the pregnancy, the better she will feel and she will be more capable of getting around without many of the normal pains.  Yoga is a great way to stay flexible and to get oxygen into the blood while improving circulation.  However, it is important that the Yoga instructor be aware of the pregnancy so modifications can be made to ensure mom and baby stay safe.

In all things, remember that keeping her first in your mind before you do anything is always a good idea. If needed, wear a WWJD (What would Jesus Do) arm band, and substitute the J for 'Joe' (Joe being the ultimate man who is completely manly but is also the ideal husband that every man resents and fear…the fear of course is that our wives would find out what a great guy he is and start asking questions like, "Why can't you be more like Joe"… oh, how I hate that Joe guy).

### Chapter 4 – Goodbye Game Room, Hello Nursery

That 56" Plasma TV hanging just perfect with the 7:1 surround placed so that all the sounds balance to the old worn leather couch in the last remaining bachelor room of the house is about to be compromised. Sure, you could probably move to the basement, down there with the furnace, cat litter and her deformed brother who prefers to live under the stairs. It is true though; the baby can't stay in a crib next to your bed until he is old enough to head off to college, so he will need his own space. And you will truly appreciate a little private time with the MILF.

You have two choices, listen to what she wants for the nursery…pastel colors, clowns or fairies, a Jinny Lind crib… or you can do something more:

Okay, maybe there is something in between. Still, you have a unique opportunity and several months to plan out the ultimate baby space. She will appreciate all the work (as she will be of little to no help here, remember there will be a big baby belly that is uncoordinated and prone to bumping you while you are hammering causing you to hit your thumb and *&!@@!). This is also a good way to get some alone time. She will want you to listen to every little thing she has researched on the internet, read in one of her books, heard from her friends or family about the baby. Sure, we love her and will love the baby...but sometimes there are just too many words that women need to survive, and we men can only take it in small doses. Give us a grunt and a two sentence summary and we get it! Kidding aside, creating the nursery is a good way to connect with your coming baby and will give you a sense of pride and a feeling like you are doing something. Be prepared, the room could cost you as much as that ideal bachelor game room did! Baby furnishings are not cheap, but if you plan ahead you can limit future costs as the baby moves to toddler and to youth.

## Plastic Crates and boards...and other furnishings

Every home has to establish a budget to work within to create a nursery. Some may need to share a room with a sibling (or you successfully negotiated for ½ of the manly game room which we all know will eventually become zilch). Others may have the money to build on to the home and custom build the space, but if you are like me and not rich, here are some basic furniture items the baby will need.

- Crib – The baby's home for the first year (a bassinette, which is a tiny crib used for the bedside when they are tiny babies, is nice to have for the first month and then discarded. If you don't have the extra cash, the crib works just fine.)

- Chair – You will need one that is comfortable and preferably rocks. There may be many nights when feeding in the room late at night is imperative. It is never recommended to fall asleep while holding the baby, but if you are sitting waiting for them to fall asleep in their crib, by all means, nap away.

- A small lamp – If you have an overhead light you won't want to turn it on at 3:00 A.M. when the baby wakes up to eat. The only thing that does is to wake them fully...then it's play time. Instead, use a small lamp that gives off 25W of light to keep the room dim and won't shock you or the baby into wakefulness.

- A small table – You need a place for the lamp, it is also a good place to put the bottle down if you are feeding and a place to hold the baby monitor.  (See electronics)

- Changing Table/Dresser – Unless you plan on sitting on the floor to change the baby, a good changing table that can double as a dresser is perfect.  It is a good place to keep everything you need to change the baby including diapers, wipes and clothes.

That's about it for required furniture.  Some alternate items could include a wardrobe to hang up nicer baby outfits, shelves, bookcases, a playpen for the nursery which is good if you don't want the baby to spend all their time in the crib and you are working in or near the room.  While you may receive some furniture as gifts at the baby shower, you should make sure you pick out the exact models you want!  If you don't receive any as gifts and need to purchase these items yourself, realize that baby furniture is not cheap!  There is nothing wrong with buying used furniture on the internet or from a thrift store.  Just be careful that there are no recalls on the item and that they are stable and free from splinters, peeling paint and the like.  Also, while it is cool to purchase vintage pieces and antiques for the baby's room, you need to consider safety and lead paint that was fine for us as kids, then again look how we turned out.  Seriously, furniture is made to a higher standard today and watchdogs are out there to try to keep our babies safe!  It is also a good idea to use an antibacterial cleaner to wipe down the entire piece of furniture before using it.

**Convertible furniture** is becoming extremely popular with dads.  These are things like cribs that will convert into a toddler bed and eventually into a full size bed.  They cost a little more than a crib, but you avoid having to buy the latter two beds as the baby gets older.  This also holds true for Changing Tables/Dressers.  Once the baby is out of diapers, you can remove the pad from the top and it's just a dresser.  The chair, small table and lamp can be used in the child's room or somewhere else as they outgrow the nursery.  If you do choose to go with convertible furniture, make sure it is something that will appeal in the long term.  I doubt your teenage child will appreciate the Purple Dinosaur or Red Hand Puppet painted on their headboard.

**Safety** – One thing to be certain of before buying new or used furniture is to check the internet for recalls.  Some baby furniture has been deemed unsafe and you don't want your child to be a statistic to save a little time.  There will be some pieces of furniture in the room that appear to be safe, yet to a child could be deadly.  Make sure to baby proof the room and the rest of the house for that matter.  Put in safety plug covers, cabinet locks, door knob covers when they get older and wall latching for large pieces of furniture.  The first items of safety are easy and common sense.  The last is something we don't think about.  If you have a large entertainment center, it probably weighs between 100 and 500 lbs and stands from 4 to 8 feet.  While it seems stable, imaging your little yard ape climbing up the cabinets and ledges (and they will) and the unit tipping over.  To prevent tipping, take a sturdy piece of fabric and screw one end to the top of the unit and, with other side taut, fasten it to the wall.

### Dadesigning and Dadecorating

Now that you've picked furniture and have imagined how things will be placed in the room, remember to use an age old decorating rule, 'Function before fashion'.  Basically, lay out the room to suit the need of the room making it easy for you and mom to come in, pick up, feed, change and put the baby back to bed. You may need to move the crib so when the door opens the light from the hall doesn't shine straight into the crib, or that the chair isn't placed dead center of the room making it easy to trip over in the dark.

What color is best? Yellow is bright and sunny and should give the child a good disposition. Blue is calming and relaxing. Dark colors are soothing and lull babies to sleep. Light colors give children energy and make them happy. Flowers, photos, Paintings and drawings attract the eye, and can be interesting for the developing child, but the question of taste can be an argument between you and your significant other. You want cars, sports or fishing themed in the room, she wants flora, fauna or something pastel as the theme. As much as word compromise is thrown around, the plain fact is that only one of you can win. One option is to do it the way you want and surprise her; if she hates it you can always procrastinate changing it until it grows on her. Again, she may procrastinate giving you any until you do. The other option is to listen to her and do what she likes. If your home is like 98% of others in this county, she will win. (That doesn't mean you can't hide a small Jaguar logo painted tastefully behind the changing table. She needn't ever know it's there.)

Make sure the paint or wall paper you choose is not toxic as babies will lick, chew and play with the walls. This is true for just about everything in your house, so make sure you consider everything as edible to these little creatures. If something looks questionable, put it out of reach of a child.

If you choose to wallpaper, you will find that it can be an expensive undertaking with questionable results. With paint, if you don't like the color it is easy and relatively cheap to paint over. Wall paper looks nice but would require stripping. You may want to visit a decorating center that has a computer that can show what your room would look like if you wallpapered.

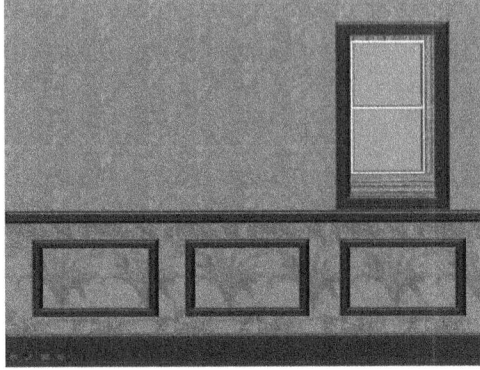

If you an amateur painter or paper hanger, don't fear, it's easier than it looks. Many home centers offer small classes on painting and wallpapering with some quick advice on how to deal with challenging areas. If you are uncomfortable doing either, try painting. The worst that could happen is that you or someone else will have to paint again.

Pictures and wall hangings can improve the look of your space. Remember to keep the items out of reach of baby! The first thing they will do is pull them down. If you are going to hang pictures, make sure they are secured to the wall solidly so they don't accidently fall. What you hang is another 'negotiation' that you will likely find is more of a mandate. One key to remember is to look at what you intend to hang on the walls before painting or wallpapering to make sure the colors coordinate.

Flooring or carpeting is another ongoing debate among designers. Some will recommend carpeting to cushion the steps so that if you sneak in to peek at the baby you are less like to wake her. Also, once the baby starts climbing out of his/her crib (and they will), if they fall it will help act as a cushion. Other designers will tell you that hardwood floors with rugs are more practical and offer wonderful aesthetics to a space. To change the feel of the room, the rugs can be changed out to colors or patterns making the space new and interesting. Children are messy and can throw up, urinate, spit and a wealth of other lovely things that would need to be scrubbed off a carpet. With small area rugs, simply pick them up and throw them in the washer. If it lands on hardwood, a little soap and water will do the trick. If you don't have a choice and have carpet, you can still use small rugs to enhance the space and protect the carpet from baby puke.

## SURVIVAL TIP

**Surviving Pregnancy TIP: Mixing Paint**

Today you can get every color in the rainbow simply by taking a sample of the color you want. Computers can read the color and determine how to mix the paint in order to dry at the same tone and hues. In choosing Gloss, semi-gloss and flat paint, the question is always mess. If it is something that is going to be touched a lot, it needs to be gloss, rarely if ever should it be flat. Glossy paints allow for easy clean up with a wet rag and water. They are typically used for wood trim and bathroom and kitchen ceilings. Semi-gloss is typically used in childrens rooms and playing and living areas. These are nice but reflect a lot of light. Flat looks the best on walls, but when they get dirty you either repaint or live with it.

**Survival Tip: Escaping from Mud/Quicksand**

It is hard to imagine in this day and age that quicksand is still a concern. As rare as it may be in civilized countries, mud is quite common. I watched the news following hurricane Katrina and witnessed a woman waist high in mud. The technique to extricate yourself from quicksand is the same rule for mud. First, don't struggle. That will only wear you out and settle you deeper into the mud. It is a little unnerving to do, but the best bet is to lay backward and try to distribute your weight evenly across your body. Slowly slide yourself backward and ease your legs and feet up until you are lying mostly on top of the mud. You shouldn't sink too deep but you will be partially submerged. Make small snake like moves toward the edge of the mud, use your arms in a fan motion to help guide your movement. Move slowly. If you start to sink, resettle your weight and continue on until you are free.

## Chapter 5 - The fun stuff:  Electronics, Equipment & Gear

The joy of any man's world is to play with electronic devices.  It's been argued that any device with a remote control is marketed specifically to men.  In truth I have over a dozen remotes and most I don't remember what they go to.  Now unless you intend to have a Borg child, the need for extensive electronics with lights, whirring and spinning action will likely just over-stimulate the baby.  However, there are certain key elements that are a must:

Monitors range from low tech (a string tied to the sock and the other end to a series of bells) to very high tech (video monitoring in a hand held unit with breathing recognition as well as motion and sound).  The costs of course increase as the options improve, in other words the cooler it is the more it will cost you!  The tried and true monitors allows you to plug one end in the baby room and the sound is transferred to a handheld unit via radio waves.  Higher end models can also show you a video feed.  The hottest models now also include vibration in the event someone is vacuuming.

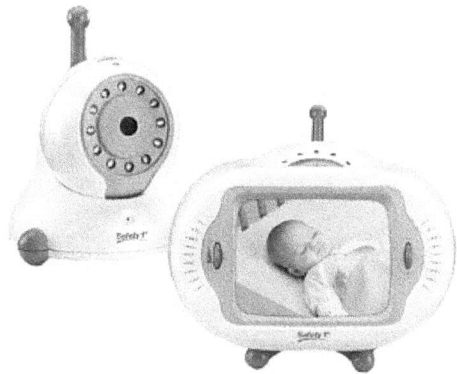

Young children commonly get about 6 to 8 colds and upper respiratory tract infections each year. Increasing the air moisture is a common way to help your child feel better when he is congested. In general, a cool mist vaporizer or humidifier is preferred over a steam or warm mist one because of the risk of your child getting accidentally burned.

Types of Humidifiers

Types of portable humidifiers include those that are ultrasonic, producing a cool mist by ultrasonic sound vibrations, or impeller humidifiers, which use a high-speed rotating disk or fan to make the mist. Both are known to disperse materials, such as microorganisms and minerals, from their water tanks into indoor air. Evaporative humidifiers, which use a fan to blow air through a wick or filter, do not.

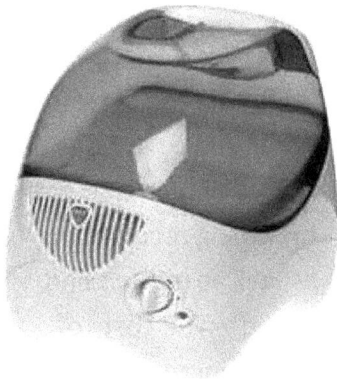

Tap Water or Distilled

Humidifiers can disperse minerals into the air, and so it is usually best to use distilled water in your humidifier. Tap water contains many minerals, and if used, can cause a white dust to coat surfaces in your house, and scale to develop inside your humidifier, which can be a breeding ground for microorganisms.

## Germs

In addition to dispersing minerals, humidifiers can disperse germs into the air. To minimize this from happening, be sure to follow the manufacturer's directions, and clean your humidifier regularly. Humidifiers can also increase dust mites and mold in your house, and should be avoided if your child has an allergy to dust mites or mold.

## Hidden Costs

Many humidifiers need replacement filters or wicks. Knowing the cost of these replacement items and how often they have to be replaced can help you find the 'true' cost of your humidifier.

## Lights, Sounds and other Fun Electronic Toys...

Okay, now it's man time. Get some wires, lights, electronics and we are set to go. When thinking through the baby's room you may think, 'hmm, wouldn't it be neat if he could see stars at night when he wakes up?' and you'd probably be right in concept. Practicality dictates certain actions... punch a hole through the ceiling and put in a sky light. Of course then we are talking about structural work to your house, and if you rent that would not be so cool. Of course you would also need to consider blocking the light in the day time and it just gets messy from there. Another option is to use fiber optic or led lighting to create a star field. The process is simple, but will take a lot of time.

You will need the following: an illuminator, a cable, a drill with .75mm, 1mm and 1.5mm drill bits and any type of glue that will give you about 20 minutes of "work time". You also MUST have access to the ceiling from the top and bottom to install the cable. The first thing you will have to do is measure how large the star field will be and where the illuminator will be locate; you will have to service the illuminator eventually. These two things are critical for a successful project! An average starfield will have 4 or so "stars" per square foot. You can go higher or lower than this, but remember that you will probably want to double, or even triple, some of the strands to create a true night sky effect.

After it's been determined how many stars you want, you can figure out how long the cable needs to be. Remember that the cable is the most expensive part of a star field and try to keep the runs to a minimum. Example: For a 10-foot by 10-foot square star field we would want about 400-450 stars. We can go with six runs of cable, four 8-foot pieces of 75-strand, one 6-foot piece and one 4-foot piece. You have to add a service loop to the illuminator for each length of cable.

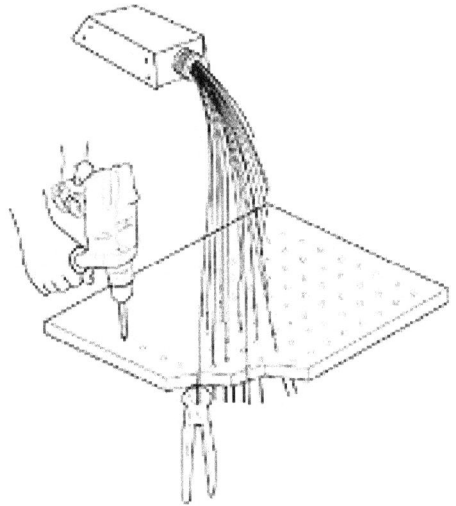

Working with two people, one below the ceiling and one above, you can now start the installation. You will have to strip the cable jacket from the strands of cable near where you will want to install the stars. You don't have to strip the entire run of cable. The person below the ceiling will drill a hole where he/she feels a star should go, the person above will shove one, two or three strands (depending on the size hole drilled) of cable through the ceiling – about 3 inches is fine. Put a small amount of glue (silicon or Liquid Nails but NOT Tite Bond) on the cable to hold it in place. Do not snip the cable at this time. Go to the next one and repeat. Try to leave a few strands from each cable free so that you can fill in any bare spots. Also, try and leave a path for you to work from and start from the furthest point of your star field – leaving an exit for yourself. The illuminator may be placed in a ventilated attic but it will reduce the lamp life and the illuminator could get hot.

After you have completed the star field, you may now paint the ceiling or prepare it in any way you wish. After this has been done, snip the strands with a scissors about ¼ inch from the ceiling. This will allow you to paint the ceiling again at a later date.

If you have a drop down ceiling, remove one of the ceiling tiles and work on an adjacent one. If you are working with sheetrock that hasn't been installed yet, place the strands in the sheetrock like you would a regular ceiling, leaving a place for the mud to go. Leave strands for later when you can fill in these empty places.

IMPORTANT  Leave an 18 Inch loop of cable at the end of the illuminator in case you need to service it.

IMPORTANT  You must polish the cable end that goes into the illuminator. If you don't, the light output will be weak and you could actually melt the cable (one good reason to have a service loop in the cable!).  Also, if the cable ends are not trimmed before you insert the harness you could damage or destroy the twinkle wheel!

If you want a less expensive and easier project, there are light kits that utilize long life LEDs that run cool and are simple to install. You may want to consider installing a temporary faux ceiling if you don't want to damage your ceiling or if you are renting and cannot make structural changes. Fiber optic and led lighting is relatively expensive and while it creates an incredible look to a room, you may want to work small scale first to see how it will look and if you can pull it off.

Another idea to add to your star field is to hang planets, moons and comets from the ceiling so that they face down. Also, don't forget when spacing your stars to create nebulas and other normal astronomical designs. This project is fun and worthy of taking your time to do it right. Remember, never attempt to work with electrical items if you are unfamiliar or uncomfortable doing so.

**Nightlights** are great ideas for the parent as well as the child. We often think that the baby will need a light in case they wake up and it's dark. Let's ponder this for a moment...didn't they just live in a dark place for 9 months? Babies don't mind the dark as much as we do. However, nightlights are great for parents. When we need to go into the baby's room in the middle of the night, we won't need to turn a light on, thereby waking the baby fully. The night light usually gives off enough illumination to see your way around the room, and if your eyes can adjust to the light, you can easily feed and rock the baby back to sleep.

Other gift items you may receive may include a device to hang inside the crib that lights, plays music, nature or heartbeat sounds and some can even vibrate. As you baby gets older it is a good idea to have such a device as it helps soothe and ultimately will lull the baby to sleep. There is some speculation that a baby will sleep more comfortably if it hears a heartbeat, again that's all the baby heard for 9 months and it would stand to reason that the same sound should be found relaxing. These devices typically run on batteries and attach to the crib rail with plastic straps. The units normally shut off automatically to save on battery life and can be activated by the baby. Find one that has volume control and options for lights and sounds.

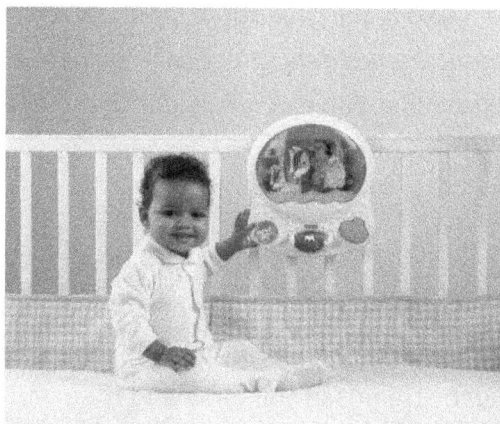

The key to having a child who will sleep soundly is to live life normally! You don't need to turn the television down, wait to cut the grass, vacuum the carpets or listen to the radio. The baby has heard noise for months before delivery so it won't mind it if you make some now. If you create a 'quiet' environment, the baby will get used to that and will have difficulty sleeping if you make noise. While the crib sounds are nice, there is no reason you can't wire in some baby room surround sound and pipe in some soft, classical music or other music from a CD player. You then have complete control over what the baby hears. Also, at 3am, you don't want to listen to Twinkle, Twinkle little Star from the crib music device for the one hundredth time! There of course is no need to blast the tunes. That will just agitate the baby and may have the opposite effect of having a quiet house…to get to sleep the baby will need lots and lots of noise.

Alright this section talked about other neat toys, and lets be real here…babies don't have really neat toys… all they can do is watch things. It's up to your own ingenuity to create neat things for them. Consider making a mobile from old CDs or your favorite actions heroes. (Also make sure you keep it out of baby's reach and that the items are securely attached). Perhaps someday when your child is older you can finally get that megalithic Star Wars Lego set you've been eyeing at the toy store.

**Lights, Camera…Action**

Previously we discussed baby monitors with the ability to capture and transfer video streams of the baby and their activity. This is a great real time activity, but is limited in scope. Consider installing a web cam into your baby's room that can be brought up on any television in your home, and even create an IP to view it from your computer at work. This is now more common in daycare and nursery centers as more and more parents want to know what goes on when they are not around. It's not quite like having a nanny cam, but it can surely serve a similar purpose. This of course is getting into some technical knowhow which can be found on the Free Advice section of my website www.daddysurvivalguide.com . A recommendation would be that if you pursue this option, invest a little more money so as to allow you remote maneuvering of the webcam such as pan and zooming functions.

**SURVIVAL TIP**

**Survival Home Tip:  Wires and Electricity**

Get your house baby proof now.  The baby won't be crawling for a while, but when they do it's just one less task.  Be sure to look at wall sockets, wires and other hazards that a baby will likely get in to.  Once they are crawling, they will look and explore everything in their reach. If you have a lamp plugged into the wall, the baby will try to pull the plug out and possibly pull the lamp down on themselves.  Place obstacles in front of wires and outlets with things plugged into them. Also, use plug protectors that automatically shut when something is unplugged.  Tie up wires and tuck them away from the baby's reach.  If you have a number of speaker and cable wires coming from your home entertainment system, you can use Velcro straps to tie them together.  Always remember: Safety first!

**Survival Tip: How to Make Electricity**

It is very unsafe to play with electricity, but if you need to wire a radio to an alternate power supply because your batteries ran out, this is a fun and interesting exercise. You will need a lemon, a paper clip, a piece of 18 gauge copper wire and a small flashlight bulb.

1.      Roll the lemon to agitate the insides
2.      Straighten out and insert the paper clip into one side of the lemon
3.      Stick the copper wire into the other side of the lemon, make sure the ends don't touch
4.      Touch both metals to the electrical points of the flashlight bulb, it should light.

You would obviously need more lemons, wires and paperclips to link together for more power, but this is an easy project for any man.

Prior to the baby coming, you will need to make sure you have a good digital camera and digital video camera. Don't attempt to do both on one device. While many devices today tout that they can do both, there is usually a trade off one way or the other. Some DV cameras have an extra memory card that you can snap a photo to using the same lens and zoom features as the video feed, however they are typically not easy to maneuver and flash is typically not available. Cameras that do video are typically limited to how much they can store and the video is usually choppy and grainy. That's because cameras lack some basic video elements.

Regular cameras are a thing of the past and should be left there. They are limited to how many photos that can be taken and you can never be sure if you got the photo or not. There are some newer 35mm cameras that have a digital screen that allows you to see the photo as you take it, but this hybrid would benefit by including a digital memory card so you could choose whether it's going to be a standard 35mm or a digital photo. Make sure you have fresh batteries, a fresh memory card or two that will allow 100+ photos (you may not have time to download images for a while after the baby is born), and that it is on you packing list for the hospital. For a DV video device, make sure you have a clean tape or disk inserted and that you have plenty of extras on hand. This too should be put on the packing list for the hospital and if you plan on recording the delivery, make sure this is in the bag you take in while she is having the baby. (You can read more about packing lists later in this chapter.) As batteries will discharge energy even when the devices they power are not in use, it is a good idea to recharge weekly.

Let's talk about recording the delivery. You have the video camera out and recording as the soon to be baby mama is in a wheel chair on her way to the birthing room and the question comes up, 'how much of this are you going to get?'. If you ask her, all of it, after all she expects that you packed extra batteries, tapes, and can hold the camera the whole time. You think, '... this is going to be hours of useless video'. Sure, you could set up the camera on a tripod and attach a power cord to get the 'entire' event, or you can record on and off through the delivery process. The latter is much easier to edit into something someone might actually want to sit through. Make sure to record any parts where she cusses you out for doing this to her, and that she is going to rip your lips off if you say, 'shh, it's okay sweetie'. You will want this footage later as she will forget ever doing it, and it is excellent retaliation when you have an argument that you are bound to lose. Simply play the video and tell her how hurt you felt when all you wanted to do was tend to her needs. It doesn't always work, but it is good for about 70% of the inescapable situations that you as a man will get into.

Now here is the real question; do you want to record the delivery itself? Full on crotch shot, bad lighting and more hair than on my cousin Paulee. Sure, its' natural it's been done for eons this way, and for a man quite disturbing. First, think about your audience. I sat through the video of a friends baby, well actually an acquaintance of my wife's, and for an hour and a half I only had a view of the woman's crotch. When the baby's head started to come out, I had enough... you might as well have asked me to watch a cow make poo. The point to this story is that you don't know who might watch the video later, and you may want to consider hiding it with the other videos that you made with your significant other during the original baby making process. There are other less obtrusive ways to make the video, shot at an angle from the mother's head so you only see the baby coming out for example, but it is not really the same experience. The mommy will want to see what you saw as it was happening, so again you may be stuck here. Look at it this way, when your child is a teenager, this is a great tool to use when talking about sex or as punishment to watch their mother giving birth to them.

There are key elements during delivery that you will want to record including the head coming out, the baby all the way out, the mommy and of course you in the shot every so often so you can prove you were there during the delivery of the baby. (She will forget just about everything that day).

It is equally important to carry along the digital camera, but there will be plenty of time later to take still photos. It's probably best to wait until the baby is cleaned and swaddled, then start snapping photos of mommy holding him or her for the first time, you holding the baby for the first time...and the lovely thing about the digital imaging age is the picture taking will never stop. There is something so cute about a small wrinkly little thing that everyone wants to snap tons of photos, then torture their friends with non-stop sharing.

The following is a sub-list of items you need to be sure you carry along:

- Digital Camera

- Rechargeable batteries for the digital camera

- Charger to recharge the batteries

- Extra flash memory cards for the camera

- Digital Video Camera

- Fully Charged Battery Pack installed in DV Camera

- Extra battery pack

- Power Cord

- Extra media (DVD or Tape)

- Tripod to be used on either camera

It is important that this be part of the bag that you take in during the delivery. Make sure you mark your bag as well as all your equipment.  You'd be surprised how many people forget these things once that little wonder pops out.

## Chapter 6 - Clothes, Car Seats & Caribous

The first thing for you to remember is that your baby is going to need clothes.  They are not born wearing a sleeper and carrying along a garment bag...although the mommy looked big enough to be carrying all that.  Now, mommy will have already thought through all this and has probably picked out some outfits for the hospital and to bring baby home.  She also received clothes from friends and family for the baby which were certainly cute and adorable.  But if you didn't pick out any outfits, it is likely you will be carrying around a little puff ball...and throw in that pink Hello Kitty diaper bag while you're at it.  Although you will not likely have a lot to say about his/her wardrobe, you definitely need to own some clothing that will cause people to remark, 'the father must of dressed the baby', or my favorite, 'I told her this would happen if she married and bred with the bastard, now their child is doomed'.  Here are some other ideas for t-shirts and onesies (t-shirts that have buttons to hold the diaper up):

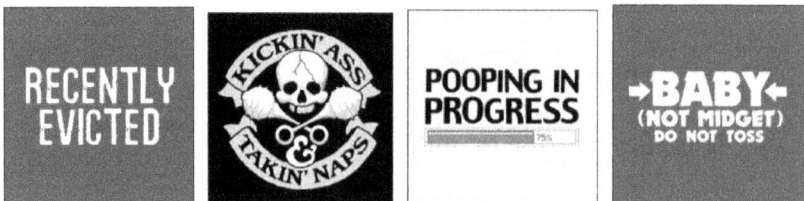

Baby clothes should be tasteful, so just bring a sweater along to cover up the shirt in the event you run into your mom at the grocery store.  Make sure to use your camera to take a picture, and if your baby's hair is long enough use a little hair gel to spike a Mohawk first.  It is likely that these outfits along with those '80's muscle pants and your favorite 'broken in' recliner will just disappear.  You ask her what happened to them, and she will reply, 'why dear you must have misplaced them, you lose everything...'  She of course will walk away smiling knowing that you are too lazy to look in the diaper trash for them.

Speaking of diaper trash, we should discuss a very important device for the baby's room:  A non-smelling, no seeing diaper pail.  There are a number of devices on the market that make it easy to dispose of poopie diapers, keeps the odors out of the living space and is easy to remove to the trash bin.  The truth is that these devices seldom work as advertised and guess who has to remove the smelly bag full of poopie diapers?  A simple low cost solution is to keep a lined trash can outside, and wrap diapers in perfumed disposable diaper plastic bags.  These can be purchased at most stores and comes in packs of 50 or more.  Simply take the poopie diaper, tie them up inside a baggie  and throw them out in the trash bin.  On trash day, take the liner out of the trash bin, spray the inside with odor eliminating spray and line it with a new bag.  Yes, they look tempting, and people will convince you to buy one, but the low tech solution in this case is still best.  (Post Note – my wife edited this book and reminded me that we did purchase a filtered diaper pail and if you use the bags and put them inside, it doesn't stink up the baby's room.  I won't admit that I was wrong, but I am thankful to only have to empty the diaper pail once a week.)

Before the baby comes home you will need diapers to fill up those smelly diaper pails.  Of course there is always a choice to go with

cloth diapers...that leak, smell and have to be rinsed out in a toilet before putting it into the laundry. Then there are the lovely disposable diapers that of course were invented by a man. If you read the instructions you are really supposed to rinse these out in the toilet as well, but do you believe anyone has ever done this? It is true that landfills have mountains of human waste in the form of disposable diapers and the only solution to keep it out is to remove the product from the market. We don't want that to happen and so we are stuck in a quandary. If you live on a farm, you can simply burn them in a fire pit and use the ash to fertilize your garden...but most of us don't live on farms (that and it's not environmentally correct to do so). So if you are like me and everyone else, you will make a compromise to recycle more so you don't feel guilty about what happens to the landfills.

Diapers come in many sizes and are made by a number of manufacturers. Some have unique designs and 'gathering' technology to reduce leaks. Others have pretty pictures on them and still others use those pictures to identify when the baby is wet. All very cool, but in the end it is the baby that will determine which one is best. Unfortunately when it comes to diapers, each child is different and their needs different. You many need to experiment with a few until you find one that works best. In the beginning you will need to stock up on **newborn** size diapers. At first, your newborn will be changed up to ten times in a day. This is because baby pee and poo are new and exciting for new parents so you feel like you need to keep them dry all the time.

This passes, by the time he/she is 18 months, you are wondering how long they can stay in a stinky diaper before the neighbors start complaining. Either way, once you find out what kind of diaper and what size you will need, buy a garage full! You will go through them all. And don't forget the wipes. Did I talk about wipes? What are wipes? Why do people call them diaper wipes? Are you supposed to wipe the diaper before putting it on the baby? No of course not. They are moist durable tissues used to wipe the baby's privates and bum. These, like diapers, need to be tested to find ones that work best for you and the baby. Some are perfumed which can be annoying after a while. You begin to associate the smell with the poopie diaper. That and babies have sensitive skin and could have a reaction to the chemicals. You might just as well smell the diaper. The thing to look for in wipes is that they come in sturdy leak proof containers, that they are dye and perfume free and that you can get smaller packs for travel. As men, we are likely to go to a big box store and buy a case of 500 wipe containers which are great! However, they are tough to fit into a diaper bag. You will argue with the baby's mother about how much more expensive the smaller packs of wipes are and attempt to negotiate a deal: If you remove a handful from the larger less expensive container of wipes and put them in a zip lock bag, you have saved at least $0.35. Over the course of the baby's time in diapers that equates to about $483.26, making your practicality logical! But will she see your reasoning? Of course not, she will complain that they are difficult take out and the handy little ones have an easy dispenser. She will also complain that you will have to load up the zip lock bag to make sure there are enough. Of course you would agree to do it and not likely ever do it, not even the first time. There is a helpful tip, and a worthy compromise...you can purchase reusable plastic wipe holders that are small making it easy to fit into a diaper bag.

They allow you to load them with wipes from your bigger container and have a lid with an easy dispenser. A win win, except that you will still not load the thing even if you buy it for her. Let's agree that at some point, you will still have to assert your manliness and she will have to accept that as a man you will overlook this task all the time...like, putting clothes into the hamper, using a napkin when eating sloppy Joes, not burping in front of the in-laws... you know, normal everyday guy stuff.

Moving on to other hardware necessary to have on hand before the baby comes. You will be enticed to go shopping for cool things only to find out later it was to take you to a baby store. Once there, your significant other will use her handy list (which she has created and said she told you about, and said she talked to you about nearly a hundred times, yet you don't ever remember seeing it...although there was a time during the break in the game on T.V. that you heard something about car and seat from her as she was walking out of the room exasperated because you interrupted her non-stop talking to ask for a beer... I mean, if you didn't interrupt the constant stream of words coming from her mouth... and there it is, there was something about a baby and a list and you remember). Here is the best you can do, smile and nod. Expect to spend 3 to 6 hours wandering around a store as she points out things the baby 'must' have. The only joy you get is that before you start this process, someone hands you a handheld scanner with a digital readout. Your job, as a man, is to scan the bar code for the item. Now, this is where men and women differ greatly. The purpose of the trip is not to buy anything, but to pick out things that you would buy if you had the money. Not the cheap stuff that you'd actually buy because the baby will 'need' it. The list you now understand is a means to inform other people to buy your baby stuff that you've picked out. There will be a number of events and family gatherings where people will hand you gifts simply because you are having a baby. Not to let you down, but it is unlikely that someone will buy the baby a gift such as, let's say... a Wii™. You can try to buy one yourself and tell your significant other that there are some interactive activities that will help you learn how to feed, change and interact with the baby. I am sure someone has developed a game like that ... somewhere. In fact, I bet if you go back to where you found this book, perhaps they have one. And if you manage to pull that one off, and we actually develop such an interactive game for Nintendo™, we fully understand that it will never make it out of its packaging. That being said, it may not be as hard as we originally thought to develop the game after all. Remember, it is not a real game, it's just a prop. The disc inside will have a horrible movie that we didn't watch with Madonna in it. Nor will it be sanctioned by the wonderful people at Nintendo™, who, if for promoting their Wii™ product in my book, should really send me a Nintendo Wii™ for free. I'm not proud and I don't make much money as a writer so I could truly benefit from the promotional perks of advertising one of the newest and greatest interactive gaming systems on the market. ☺ I<3 Wii™

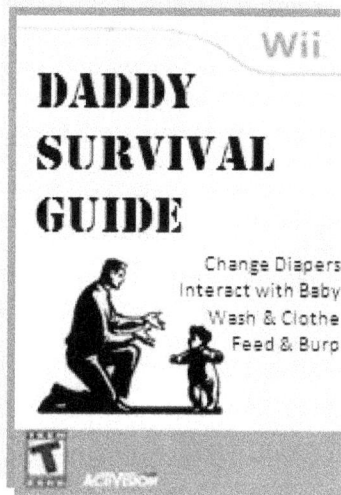

Wii

DADDY
SURVIVAL
GUIDE

Change Diapers
Interact with Baby
Wash & Clothe
Feed & Burp

ACTIVISION

# SURVIVAL TIP

**Survival Tip for Baby:  Car Seats**

A newborn needs to be secured in a car seat that has a five-point strap system.  That means that there are two shoulder straps which are usually connected to two hip straps and connect to a single crotch buckle.  There is a single red button in the middle that releases the straps for easy baby removal.  The button is a little tricky so make sure you try it out first.  It is designed to keep babies and idiots from undoing them.  Don't be an idiot, practice and understand how it works.

Next, the car seat should be placed in the center back seat of the car facing toward the back window.  If you were to get into a front end accident, this is the best position for the infants' body to survive the impact.  The car seat instructions will tell you how to connect the seat belt and attach the extra security strap.

**Survival Tip:  Perform a Controlled Skid**

You're James Bond and the only way to fit into that parallel parking spot is to slide in sideways.  This takes a little practice and a very good emergency brake.  While pressing on the gas, turn your wheels hard to the left while holding up your emergency brake, this will turn your car sideways, let off the gas and turn into the skid until you come to a stop.  You may need to practice this one for a while.  We don't recommend doing it, you could poke your eye out!

## Car Seats

You will likely have 'registered' (that is the bar coding thing you did earlier) for one of these. The ones most people get are plain, but are designed to do the job. The key elements to a car seat include forward and backward facing ability, a five point strap system, extra security strap, easy adjustment and easy release features.

Forward and backward facing allows your child to grow without having to get a new seat. Typically the first car seat you will have will be small to match the size of the baby. The car seat will also likely have a base that separates from the main unit so it can be carried. This is quite convenient as you don't need to unstrap the baby from the car seat and it's easy to take the baby with you and have a place to keep them contained if you are visiting family or going to the grocery store. It's too bad they don't come in teenager sizes. When the baby is small, it does not have control over his/her neck and head and must be handled delicately. By placing the seat backward, the forward and stopping movement of the car is less impactful on the baby's neck. Laws vary by state on age or weight as to when you can turn the car seat around.

If you do your homework, you can find that there are convertible car seats that can be removed from the car and placed into a stroller with ease. These are often referred to as travel systems. What I find most incredible is that they are designed to be locked into most styles of shopping carts in that pull out area where you often see toddlers sitting. It is a good idea that if you have more than one car, to buy an extra base to allow for the easy movement from car to car, car to stroller, car to shopping cart and back to car and carrying baby to house... preferably where someone will take the baby out of the car seat, feed him/her, change him/her and put him/her down for a nap...and that someone not being you.  Since it is unlikely in this universe, at least it's easier to carry the baby into the house.

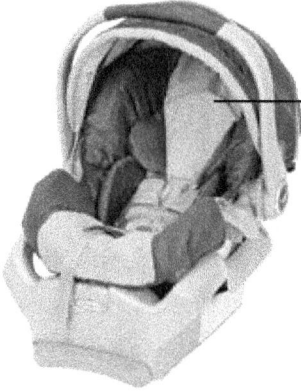

5 Point Strapping System

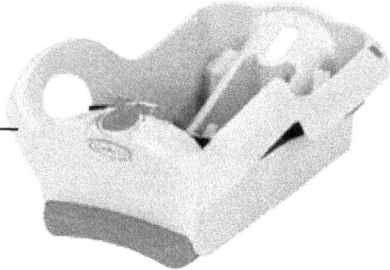

Additional Base

Carrier Stroller

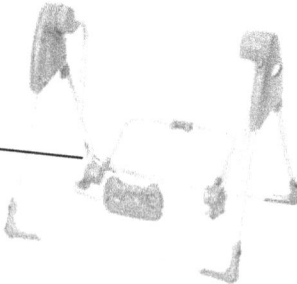

Carrier Swing

When you go to the hospital to pick up the baby (and the mommy of course, someone has to feed and clothe the baby) you will need a car seat. It is likely the hospital will want to inspect it first and will give you instructions on how to put the baby into and out of the car seat. They will remind you to place the car seat in the back seat facing the rear. They may also tell you to get a head cushion. This is a little piece of foam and fabric that goes around the baby's head so it doesn't roll around. Again, once the baby is able to sit on their own, they really don't need this anymore. When not in the car, be careful not to leave the baby in the car seat all the time. It can be a temptation because it's comfortable for the baby who was used to being balled up in his/her mommy's belly, but the baby needs to learn to stretch which is crucial for muscle development.

If you have a small car, a small baby will become a big problem with all the gear that goes along with him/her. You will need the car seat and base of course. If you plan to walk around, you must take a stroller. Carrying babies are cute, but after 10 minutes they are hot and heavy! Trust me, you want to work smart, not hard. If you need to show the baby off, pull him/her out of the stroller and when finished, put the baby back. See, simple. Now, while most strollers fold up, they don't disappear and leave quite a large footprint. So keep your trunk

clear. You will also need to carry a diaper bag. These can be bulky, but everything the baby needs from food, to diapers to clothes to a cheese steak sandwich are going to need to be carried wherever the baby goes. The sustenance is to rebuild your strength, because after lugging all this stuff around you will begin to wonder, "why do we bother going out at all?"

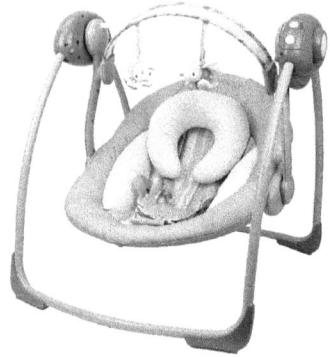

If you intend on staying some place for a while, you may also want to take along a portable playpen for the baby to lie in. Again, don't leave the baby in the car seat for hours on end. Think how uncomfortable you would feel if the roles were reversed. These devices fold up fairly well and again leave a moderate size footprint for your trunk. If you intend to have the baby up and active for a while, you may want to include a baby activity center or some toys. Would you take your dog to the park and not bring a tennis ball or Frisbee? But if the baby is fussy, you either will be walking and rocking the baby, or pack along a portable baby swing or bouncy seat. Swings are from the gods! The reason my daughter lived to go to college is because we had one. Can you say lifesaver? After days with minimal sleep, we learned that by putting her in the swing, it mimicked us carrying and rocking her. Wind it up and there you go. Another caution: use the swing sparingly...only when you can't hold or rock the baby. Rules apply the same for the swing as the car seat. Bouncy seats are a nice switch up from the car seat in that they aren't as bulky and allow the baby to move around much freer and of course it bounces. Some come with lights and other fun things to watch and touch. When the baby starts eating baby food it's a nice alternative to using a high chair.

And of course now that we've gotten to high chairs, there are a few key elements to look for:

**Highchair Fundamental Elements**

(1) Adjustable back to accommodate infant to toddler

(2) Seat straps to keep the little ankle biters from escaping

(3) Removable tray to allow for a quick wash down...these get messy... get an extra one if you can

(4) Wheels that can lock.  You will move the highchair around a lot, and then to be safe you will want to lock it in place... safe because if that kid keeps scooting his chair closer to the oven he will be eating spinach and carrots for a week.

(5) A foot tray.  Most people think this is to keep the feet from just dangling... and that is functionally the truth, but they are also great at catching the food that somehow finds its way over the edge of the tray...pretty much all the time.

Okay, so I did promise a caribou as implied by the title of this section.  I don't hunt caribou; I find the meat a little gamey.  But I do like to use it as a reason to take a break.  Both you and mommy need to take a break from time to time...to go to the movies, to go to dinner, to go caribou hunting.  You need to separate yourself from the baby once in a while... for a few recuperative hours to help remember why you decided to add a new life to your family.  My favorite break time is to plan for a long, late evening, dropping the baby off at the sitters... rushing in the car through the fast food drive-thru and then back home for a two hour nap!!  Yes, more could have been done in that time, but believe me...the sleep will be much better. Don't forget to set an alarm and pick up the baby.

CARIBOU WITH BIG PLANS...

**Shopping list summary:**

- Something for the baby to wear home from the hospital (make sure to include a blanket and hat)

- Cool clothes that you can dress the baby in

- Carrier/Car Seat with Base

- Stroller – the kind that will accept a carrier/car seat

- Diaper Bag, Newborn Diapers & Wipes

- Bottles/Nipples (We didn't talk about this yet, so if you were just scanning to get to this list you didn't miss anything.)

- Swing – both portable and full size

- Bouncer (No, not Bruno at Club Risque)

- Play Pen aka Pack n Play™

- Digital Video Camera, Digital Camera & Rechargeable batteries (Getting Déjà vu?  We did talk about this part of the list already)

- Pacifier (We didn't talk about these, that's the mommy's job and let's just leave it at that)

- Nintendo Wii™ complete system with Guitar Hero … and the Daddy Survival Guide ;-) for educational purposes of course.

- High Chair, Diaper Pail and a Cheese Steak Sub

## Chapter 7 - Nipples...this is the X-rated section

Ha! Made you look! This is where we will talk about that ever important place on a woman that is no longer your personal domain. You have two choices in supporting your woman: Be a guy or be a man.

**Be a guy:** Her breasts have grown quite large over the pregnancy and you are all excited to think that she will lose the baby weight and those fun bags are going to stay. Guess what...if you read the earlier part of this book I tell you that they go away.. or get smaller at least. They got big in the first place because they were preparing to make milk...yeah, like a cow and every other mammal on this earth. So, those large breasts will expel milk. Not so inviting anymore are they? Not only that but if she breast feeds, that kid is going to be latched to them all the time making them less sensitive and making you impatient for the day that the baby stops breastfeeding. Now, in the hospital a shot can be administered if the mommy chooses not to breast feed. This will tell the body to not make milk. Everything goes back to the way it was prior to the pregnancy...for the most part. Obviously some things change. Upside for this option, you get your boobs back all to yourself. Downside, they lose their size.

**Be a man:** The La Leche League has helped fund extensive studies to prove that breast milk is better for the child's development over formula. Even the companies that make formula will agree. Tests show that women who breast feed have children who score 10 points higher on IQ tests. I am not sure how skewed the statistical analysis is on the test base for it would seem to me that women who make an informative decision to breast feed are usually more intelligent and those genes pass on through to the baby. Either way, it is true that breast milk is best. Upside, great cleavage...downside, milky boobs.

Not to be overlooked, babies who breast feed are protected by the immunities their mothers carry and so they get sick less. Also, they poo less and the poo is believe it or not...less stinky. I have done my own study having only one child that was breast fed and I can attest to the fact that bottle fed baby poo is stinky!.

There are many factors to consider when choosing whether or not to breast feed, and every person needs to make their own best choice here. Some women will try to breast feed only to find that it is neither comfortable nor productive. It does take time for the milk to come in and for the nipples to become accustomed to being drawn upon to feed a growing infant. Eventually, it works. It did for millions and millions of years... you and I are proof, whether we were breast fed or not. Of course in the old days, a king could have his wife use a wet nurse to feed the baby so he didn't have to deal with milky breasts. If the baby doesn't supple, eventually the breasts will stop producing milk. A wet nurse is today's version of formula, an alternative to the mommy giving milk from her own body. Formula today provides essential nutrients and simulates the milk the mother would get, so if she can't breast feed, it's not a big deal and nothing to stress over. However, once you turn the spicket off it won't come back on. If she stops breast feeding and the breasts stop producing milk, they will not start producing again unless she becomes pregnant. So you can't try formula for a while and switch over to breast milk. You can however try breast milk and switch to formula later on. Just be aware that the baby's stomach is sensitive to changes and may have gas or other bad reactions to being switched.

Breast pumps sound like fun. But they're not. They are not even that interesting. The challenge is that once the milk starts coming, it wants to keep coming. It will leak from the breasts forcing the mommy to wear special absorbent pads to keep from leaking through her blouse. It can also cause discomfort to the mother if she doesn't feed the baby every few hours. So, while not exciting, breast pumps are very useful tools to store up milk for the baby in the event mommy is not around or you are out in public. They are also very helpful in relieving the pain of engorged breasts.

On a side note, some people will tell you that if a baby is sleeping not to wake them up. They believe that when a baby is hungry they will wake up and cry to let you know. The same is true when they are wet. Yeah, as a long time dad I can tell you that if you want to keep your baby on an even keel, get them on a feeding and changing schedule. It is not good for a small baby to go for long periods of time without eating. They do not possess fat stores and can dehydrate quickly. If you smell strong urine, soft spot or sunken eyes, lack of drool or no tears then you need to call your pediatrician as these are signs of baby dehydration.

Back to breasts though, again a favorite subject of mine... another reason for using a breast pump is to create a store of milk that can be bottled and used by you to feed the baby. Remember, ½ that kid is you! 50% of its genetic makeup. Some chemical bonds in the DNA strands are because of you. So you are equally responsible to bond with the baby, and that includes feeding. She may be up all night long feeding and getting very little rest, and you need to help her by sacrificing your own sleep. It will pay off later. She can't use the excuse that she had to do all the work with the baby, one less weapon in her arsenal to use against you when you come home at three in the morning after getting the worst player in your fantasy football league at your bachelor buddies house.

Breast pumps attach to the breasts and simulate the sucking motions of the baby allowing milk to be ... 'milked' from the breasts. The results get deposited into a bottle which can be stored in the refrigerator for a couple of days or frozen for a couple of months.

Important: You and your significant other want to go out and celebrate. That may include a drink or two. Unfortunately, whatever she takes into her body will get passed through her milk. That includes alcohol. No problem, just take one of the bottle from the refrigerator and feed it to the baby. The thing to remember is that she still will produce milk, even if it is tainted. The breast pump is handy here to take the milk out and dump it down the sink. Check with your doctor, but typically it will take about 2 hours for each alcoholic drink consumed which starts from the time she stopped drinking for the alcohol to leave her system, so make sure you have enough bottles in the refrigerator to accommodate the time off the breast. This also means you will need to practice bottle feeding and trying out different nipples. Babies are fussy and will prefer one type over another. It is possible that the baby will prefer a specific nipple over the mother's breast. If this happens, you may want to invest in a very good breast pump. It is not a reason to stop giving breast milk.

This section does address the need to look at and identify what kind of breast pump to use. There are electric and manual. There are ones that can pump one or both breasts at a time. Some feed into disposable bags while others pump into bottles. Discuss, do some research, talk to your doctor and other professionals about the choice to breast feed or not. Then you can add a breast pump (or not) to the registry. If you don't get one at a baby shower (not a literal, everyone get naked and into the shower kind of thing... it's a party for women, by women, and about women where gifts are given for the baby), you will need to buy one.

Regardless if you pump breast milk or formula feed you will need to buy bottles and nipples. These days there have been a lot of discussion over plastic versus glass. Some foreign studies have identified that a chemical (BPA) used in making hard plastic baby bottles can cause serious medical issues for the baby. Some people will tell you it's just hogwash (that is where they all get naked and into a shower together). Do your own research on this matter, but I will give you my own best advice.

1. It's a pain to clean bottles
2. Glass bottles break, and if you are clumsy extremely dangerous
3. Plastic bottles if not cleaned will get gunk in the bottom that won't come out and eventually you just throw the thing out
4. Bottles have air in them which get sucked in by the baby when they nurse, that then gives them gas

I chose to use inserts. These wonderful little things are disposable, so all you have to wash is the nipple. They don't break and if they get left out and the milk turns to gunk, throw it out. Air can be squeezed out before feeding it to the baby to reduce gas. Why anyone would use anything different is beyond me. The technology has been out there for over 30 years. I guess some people just like washing bottles.

I am not one for product placement, but I fully endorse Avent™ disposable bottle insert system, and my endorsement doesn't come with a million dollar contract. Again, try your own avenue with bottles, this is just my favorite.

Now, if you chose to go with formula, there are many, many choices. Like everything else with babies, they will lean to one product over another. Some babies have issues with formula ingredients and may need to change to a soy based product. Again, you will need to work closely with the pediatrician to understand what to try. Once you do settle on a formula you have to make a decision on work over cost. The powder method yields the most formula but requires measuring and mixing. A daily task that is tenuous at best. The premixed cans can be poured into bottles and used, while the balance is stored in the refrigerator. Again, it is easier than powder, but more expensive per feeding. And the most expensive is the bottle ready where all you need to do is screw a nipple on the top and feed. These are kept at room temperature...simply open and screw on a nipple...no muss, no fuss and you are ready to feed the baby. Some will try a mix and match of options, powder for every day feeding, cans for late night feedings and ready-made for on the road. The challenge is that the mixture is not consistent, and babies tummies are very sensitive! Your best bet is to mix up a batch of powder and pour all your bottles for the day and keep them in the refrigerator. It can become part of your daily routine and is not as challenging as it appears.

Babies will not eat much at first and will require 4 ounce bottles. Later they will need 8 ounce bottles. A baby will eat about 10 to 12 times per day. Do the math and figure out how often you are planning on cleaning bottles and how many you will need to prepare in a day. (Lots and Lots)

**Chapter 8 - Making Plans for the Long Haul**

There is nothing left to do but get ready for the baby. So you think. One thing that you may need to consider is your financial stability. Now that baby is coming, it's more than just an extra mouth to feed. You need to decide if work is going to change for one or both of you. The first strain will be on the amount of maternity leave she will take, how much vacation you will take and whether or not she or you will be returning to work either in a full or part time capacity.  Some people work shifts offset from one another to avoid the daycare dilemma, but a new missing my significant other dilemma appears in its place.

First, she will need several weeks to recover.  What will her employer do for her?  Paid vacation, time off with no pay?  By law, her position must be held through the Family Emergency Leave Act.  That same law allows you to take time off for the baby.  However, the time off does not guarantee that you will get paid, it only guarantees that you can return to work.  You should plan a minimum of 6 to 8 weeks for her if she plans on returning to work.  That means you need to have 6 to 8 weeks of her normal salary stocked up to get you by in your normal lifestyle.  At first the baby won't cost much.  Most of the clothes they wear will have been gifts or purchased ahead of time.  If the baby is breast feeding, the food is taken care of.  And if you planned well, you should have diapers, wipes and bottles ready to go.  You may need to buy more diapers, wipes and if you not breast feeding, formula.  There will be several doctor visits during the first couple of months for the mother and baby and if you have co-pays or deductibles, be prepared to pay for these as well.

The next consideration is the cost of working over daycare.  If you look at your household income and expenses, making sure to factor in working costs such as clothing, food, travel…, you may find that the cost of daycare may actually be more than you bring home as disposable income.  The best way to deal with this is to create a budget.  Yes, I said it.  It is not very man like to think about or create a budget…that is unless you're an accountant type, who, by the way ,are probably not reading this book anyway. (Not to say that accountants can't be manly, they would just have a hard time in investing in a book about baby care without identifying a hard number to balance it against... like the rate of return on diapers by identifying how many and which ones to purchase compared to the ones they would have had they not read the book.)

Regardless... a simple budget will do:

## Income:

| | |
|---|---|
| My Take Home Income Monthly | $3,100.00 |
| Her Take Home Income Monthly | $2,800.00 |
| **Total Income** | **$5,900.00** |

## Critical Expenses:

| | |
|---|---|
| Rent: | $1,200.00 |
| My Car: | $ 400.00 |
| Her Car: | $ 340.00 |
| Car/Renter Insurance: | $ 220.00 |
| Gas for Cars: | $ 420.00 |
| Utilities: | $ 510.00 |
| Groceries: | $ 450.00 |
| **Total Critical Expenses:** | **$3,540.00** |

*Available Cash:*     *$2,360.00*

## Regular Expenses:

| | |
|---|---|
| Credit Cards: | $ 800.00 |
| Medical/Dental Expenses | $ 100.00 |
| Loan: | $ 300.00 |
| Dining Out | $ 300.00 |

| | |
|---|---|
| Entertainment | $ 300.00 |
| Gifts/Birthdays/Holidays… | $ 300.00 |
| **Total Regular Expenses:** | **$2,100.00** |
| Savings | $ 260.00 |
| *Available Cash:* | *$ 0.00* |

It doesn't take a CPA to figure out that based on this budget, something will have to give with any change to the family. Do you eliminate a car, cut back on savings, eat out less…these are all things to consider when planning a future budget that includes your new baby. New expense items would include:

| | |
|---|---|
| Baby Formula | $ 80.00 |
| Baby Clothes | $ 60.00 |
| Baby RX | $ 40.00 |
| Baby Doctors | $ 35.00 |
| Daycare | $ 910.00 |
| Diapers | $ 60.00 |
| Diaper Wipes | $ 30.00 |

I could go on, but it is clear that there are a number of new expenses that have never been planned for and now there needs to be money to pay for the items. Some of you may be shocked by the daycare amount; to you I say do your own research and see how close I actually am.  This is a major reason many parents opt to stay home with the baby and attempt to find other means to make money.  Like, oh, I don't know...write a book about parenting.

It is true, some expenses are short term and it may be worthwhile to cut back on things like savings and dining out, but cutting back doesn't mean cutting out altogether.  It is easy to get caught in the kid trap where parents simply cannot get out of the house because they have no money to do so.  Budget in a smaller amount and just save it until you can go out for a night.  Remember that you many need to pay and tip a sitter, so budget that in to your night out.

## Clothing – Dapper Dan/Daniella

One excellent method to save money on clothing is to shop at thrift stores, yard sales and even check out friends and families whose babies have recently upgraded to new clothing.  Too many parents are stuck on getting everything new and have a false sense in believe that you can keep the clothes clean.  I will tell you a parent's secret... baby barf is a rare base element that is impossible to remove from clothing.  Find any parent of an infant, ask to look at their child's clothes, and I guarantee you that more than half their wardrobe is stained.  It's not because the parent is careless or inept at laundry, it is just a simple truth that you cannot get most baby clothes clean.  The second consideration is the amount of time babies stay small.  Newborn are newborn for a month, 3 at the most.  Most of those cute outfits that were purchased to take photos in, take the baby out... yeah, those things with the tags still on them are now too small for the baby

and just wasted money. Smart dads like me see them all the time at yard sales and pick them up for pennies on the dollar. I just shake my head and think; I wonder if I can get them to give me the jean jacket and jeans for $1.50...

Here is what no book anywhere is going to tell you, the truth about what to dress baby in during their first months at home... First understand that you should not take the baby out of the home for 6 weeks. It is a general rule offered by most pediatricians, and it's a precautionary step to avoid other human contact that may bring disease and colds to the baby while they are still very vulnerable. So the only people seeing the baby are the ones that stop by to visit. Of those, very few will drop by more than once. I like to keep in my clothing arsenal, the 'Beauty Suit' which is a very nice outfit to put on the baby to greet guests with...this should be something without baby barf on it. I keep a little note on the outfit to identify who came by when the baby was wearing it, then I put it on before the person arrives and remove it immediately after the baby was seen in the outfit. After the first look, most people realize that if the baby is in a sleeper, they are probably getting ready to take a nap. And they would be right, babies sleep all the time. For the first three months the baby needs clothes to sleep in...and that is pretty much it. Onsies which are t-shirts with snaps that fasten under the diaper, then a sleeper with or without feet over the top of that. If the baby barfs, don't panic. Take a wet towel and wipe it off. The outfit will stain no matter what! They always do. And you really can't use more aggressive laundry detergents as the baby could be sensitive to them. Buy many outfits as you will be changing them a lot and since baby clothes need to be washed together in mild detergent, it takes a while before tiny baby clothes make a large load.

**Free is free, are you leaving that quarter on the ground?**

You've probably missed reading the entire last section except for the part that told you that you could save money by only buying onsies and sleepers as you are still thinking about the budget worksheet previously discussed. Like most single and non-childrened couples, you have probably never thought about clipping coupons, looking for deals nor hoped to find free samples of diapers. Guess, what? This is you now! The competition to get your baby dollar is huge. Diaper companies will cut you all sort of breaks to get you to be brand loyal. If you buy a certain diaper brand in the first three months, you will likely be a loyal customer as long as the baby pees in his/her didees. Not only will you find stupid-sized packs with 64+ diapers per bag, the price seems exceptionally reasonable. As the baby gets older, their butt gets bigger and it makes sense that it must cost more to make so it costs more to purchase (per unit). The smart marketing teams at diaper companies have tried to keep the price point the same while just giving you fewer diapers. They like to use fuzzy logic, like ... "oh, your baby poos and pees less as they get older", and "it's harder to pack as many units and still make it viable to sell on shelves in stores"... yeah, oh poor diaper companies. In my lifetime, I have purchased over 30,000 diapers, and that's just because I stopped counting after my second daughter. If you do the math, we are talking about 32 diapers and $16 per pack on average... or $15,000 over three years.

I digress, the fact is that there are many companies out there looking for new consumers to market who will accept brand loyalty and if they give a freebie away here and there...so be it. You best tool is the internet. Seek out events and promotions and take 100% advantage of them. Use diaper coupons whenever you can! It's the difference of paying $16 versus $14.50 for something the baby is going too poop in anyway. (Those cloth diapers aren't looking so bad now). Of course as I have stated in previous portions of this book, you should not jump between products because one item is cheaper over another, babies react drastically to change and it's worth your sanity sometimes to pay a little more.

Frustrated over the price of a pack of diapers, I decided that my sweet little angel could deal with the lower end generic diaper sold at my local grocery store. They looked the same and worked the same, yet they didn't have pictures of recognizable cartoon characters, but that shouldn't matter right? I found myself saving $6 per bag. I then also realized that my laundry and cleaning bill started to rise. The generic diapers didn't hold anything in. I might have well as tied a paper towel around her butt.

Now it is true, you can scour the internet looking for free stuff, and will have some success...but you may also find that the time it took you to get those freebies could have been 5 times more profitable if you just took a job flipping burgers for minimum wage at the local greasy burger shack.

## Seconds anyone?

There, I said it. The option of taking a second job to pay for the new baby expenses is just that...an option. You may not believe that you can afford to have a baby and support it for at least 18 years. You will find though, that you will make it through and that you may need to sacrifice here and there to make ends meet. But you must consider the following...
Your baby smiles, burps, girgles and turns over for the first time. Your wife calls you to come and look...but you can't. You're at work. It's nine hours later and she is doing it again, come see... but you can't … you are at work again. You get home, eat, take a shower and go to bed to start all over again. You tell yourself that the sacrifice is only short term and that you can catch up on the weekend. But then the weekend comes, along with it all the chores you can't get done during the week.

I commend anyone who takes a second job so the mommy need not go back to work. But you must measure what really matters to you. Spending time with your new little one, or having just a little more money... I will be honest in saying that I would have gladly accepted bankruptcy over missing my daughter walk for the first time, or to giggle at me after I read her a book at night. I am not a rich as I'd like to be, and there are many people living just above poverty who take home more money than I do, but I have the love and care of children who will always have fond and loving memories of their dad.

Sometimes there are no choices. You have to take a second job for a short period of time to survive. Then do it, better to have a live healthy and whole family than no family at all. But look at your budget closely for gaps, make the second job short term. Look for ways to earn more in your current job or seek new employment.

I worked for a great company with great pay. The benefits were adequate and I had to pay ½ of the medical insurance costs. I traveled at least one week each month which kept me from home. We made a decision that it would be better if I were home more for the kids, and not only did I manage to find a job that paid me the same salary, but did not require me to pay any share of my medical insurance. Had I not looked for that job, I never would have found it and would still be away from home and making less money.

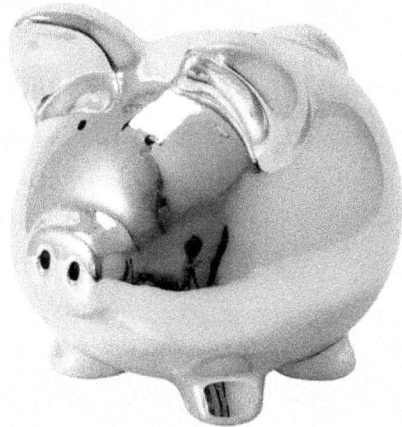

## SURVIVAL TIP

**Survival Financial Tip:  401K Plans**

You are responsible for that new little mouth, and may need to be the sole bread winner for a period of time.  This financial burden is enough to put a strain on any normal family.  But you need to remain focused on long term financial security.  As most people do not have retirement plans with their jobs these days, most companies have opted to provide 401K plans for employees to invest in the economy and plan for their own retirement.  As an enticement, most employers offer to match some of your funds.  Sounds too good to be true...?  It's true.  If you put in a dollar and the company matches 50%, they just gave you 50 cents for doing nothing at all.  In other words, free money.  There is usually a cap, like 4% of your annual income and no more than the government ceiling of $16K per year, but if I earn $50K per year, I can pay in $2K that will be matched 50% by my employer...or $1K.  So I saved a total of $3,000 for my retirement.  It comes out in small chunks from your paycheck so it's not very noticeable and as it is taken out pretax it is even less noticeable.  Instead of $2K off the top, it is actually $1,600 out of my take home pay.

**Survival Tip:  Balance a Quarter on its Side**

Challenge your buddies to balance a quarter on its side without touching it.  It must stay up for more than 20 seconds to count.  After they fail miserably, bet a dollar that you can do it.  Once they pay up, and make sure you get the money first, put the quarter on its edge and hold it with your finger, then flick it with a finger on your other hand to get it to spin on its edge.  If you practice for a while, you can easily get it to stay up for more than 20 seconds.

**Where have all the scholarships gone...?**

That sounds like a very sad folk song, but it does bring up the concern about advanced education. Kids cost a lot, there is no doubt about that. As they get older they cost more. When the leave home they don't ask for money as often, but they will ask...and this time it will be for more and for bigger things. "Dad, can you help put a deposit on our home"? If you know me, my response would be "Sure, I will put a dollar in this here piggy bank which is a gift from me to you. Put enough of those dollars in there and in no time, you have your deposit."

My dad would always talk about making wise investments for your future. Probably the best book he ever gave to me was called, 'The Richest Man in Babylon', which is more like a parable than a novel. It's about a young man who is given money by his father as he goes out to seek his own way in the world. He experiences the life lessons given to him by his father over the years and makes his fair share of mistakes. After losing everything, he rebuilds his wealth by saving small, making smart calculated investments and over a long time became... the richest man in Babylon.

You don't need $100,000 in the bank when the baby is born to ensure they have the money they need to go to college. You also cannot trust that your child will be gifted, smart, and talented enough to get a full board scholarship. Do you have to pay for your child's education? Let's review quickly, as they get older they ask for more money. If they are making more money sooner because they have a good job which was the result of a good education, they will not ask for as much money. Long term, if you help them through college, it will cost you less in the long run, it's just simple math.

So, you say that there is no room in the budget. You already cut savings back to nothing, you already don't ever go out with your significant other, and you have taken up to selling vegetables road side. I don't often recommend a business or brand, (unless they give me a large endorsement check...and by the way that hasn't happened yet) but I do like the UPromise plan. It costs nothing to join, you don't pay any money...ever. And they give you money for your child's college. How, you say? If you use your credit/checking charge card when you pay for something at certain stores, you will receive a certain percentage of what you paid deposited into an account for your child.

Math time again... Over the next 18 years, I plan to use my credit card at least 2 times a week. 1 time for gas at $45 and 1 time for dinner at $65 per week... 1% of those purchases will be deposited into my daughter's savings through UPromise. That's $1,030 for me doing absolutely nothing other than living like I already do. This of course is a very conservative amount, and over time the total will likely be between $2,500 and $5,000. The beauty is if you can get other people to use UPromise on their credit cards to benefit your child.

Secure investments by way of a passbook is good, my grandparents did it for me and put aside $5 per week which received all kinds of compounded interest. By the time I was 18 I had $6,000. Another sound investment is to purchase government savings bonds. A $25 investment for a $50 face value bond which is actually equal to $50 in 9 years, compounds nicely if held longer. If I purchased one on the day my daughter is born, on her 18th birthday that bond is worth 160% of what I paid for it. Again, a small investment can pay off big long term.

Remember that saving for a child's college is long term and investments need to be stable and if they are low producers, they can still offer a nice nest egg when it is time to fly the nest.

Lastly, there are always scholarships out there. Start looking at requirements when your child is in 9<sup>th</sup> grade. Don't overlook the little ones. A $500 scholarship will pay for a semesters worth of books. That is $500 that is not out of your pocket. And remember, it should be your child's job to find those scholarships. Some kids won't want to do it, will insist that they are not going to college, don't feel like they will fit it. Whatever you need to do to get them to do the work...do it. Having paid my own way through college with help from my Uncle Same (U.S. Army), cost me 8 years of service and two armed conflicts which included one flesh wound. A pound of flesh is not the best way to make it through life and if my college were paid for, I would have made up those 8 years in an internship to an executive position and probably would be running my own Enron Corporation into the ground.

My two oldest daughters attend colleges in Kentucky, and both are on full scholarships, and I would like to think that it was because I was an asshole. They still love me as always, but I am an asshole who now has some extra cash on hand for when they really need it. Like to get a bigger piggy bank to save money in for a deposit on a home...

## Chapter 9 - The News is Out... It's Eminent

If you read like most men...like most of my friends, you probably put this book down until the last month before she is due. There is no shame in that, we fully understand that you've been working and dealing with a hormone enraged woman for many months now. And until recently it didn't seem real. But now when you put your hand on her belly and rub gently whispering sweet words in her ear (I don't think calling her Budda Belly is considered sweet) you feel something punch your hand. There it is, a flashback. You are standing at the bar in some futuristic spaceship dressed in a white jumpsuit as are all your companions. Your friend has been looking ill since coming back from that space rock exploration you did earlier in the morning. It's funny, he looked like a goner, and had some squid thing stuck to his face. But now he's all better and toasting everyone, when suddenly there is a kick in his chest (or belly, who is to say) and next thing you know some flesh eating creature pops out.

That scene has scared every man with regards to pregnancy, and now that you see it moving inside you are freaking out. Sure, we know it's not an alien creature, but we also know that sooner rather than later it will be popping out and we have done little to prepare. Sure, she has been mooning over baby names and nursery ideas and has mentioned to you a million times that she needs you to get a move on, and you tell her that you will as soon as golfing season is over (it never is, but few women know that).

When a woman first finds out that she is pregnant, she will want to tell everyone she knows. The excitement is contagious and, next thing you know, everyone is congratulating you. Your job is to remind her to wait until she nears the end of her first trimester to 'spread the news'. It is very common for a woman to get pregnant and have a miscarriage in the first few weeks without even knowing it. As the months pass, it is less likely the body will discover that there is an alien living inside her and the chances of full term pregnancy improve. And yes, the body does want to abort the baby. Some of the hormones that are being produced by the woman is keeping the body stoned so it doesn't recognize the foreign thing growing in her. Smart hormones! I don't believe that by smelling her skin they will have the same effect on you.

By the third month, she will start to show and it is the time to tell family and friends. If you are lucky, some of her closest friends will put together a baby shower when she is nearing the end of her pregnancy. This is where that handheld scanner pays off. People will start to buy you gifts based on that list. We've already beaten this one like a dead horse. Remember, nowadays, men buy baby gifts too. So tell your buddies where to find imaginative gifts worthy of being a man. One place to start is www.daddysurvivalguide.com .(Okay, I know that was a shameless plug. )

You are not off the hook! You are going to be recruited by family or friends to come up with a list of people who should be invited. People to not include are your very hot ex-girlfriend, the stripper from your bachelor party and your mother-in-law (although you probably can't stop the last one from coming). Make sure you have possession of the address book and that you make sure the mommy-to-be has identified for you the people that she wants there. Remember it's supposed to be a surprise, so you need to tell her. (A little advice, know your baby mama well enough that she'd prefer to be surprised completely, then ignore my advice.) It is one of the few times that you can actually admit to a secret that you are keeping from her. Don't worry, she will act surprised at the shower... but to keep the peace, make sure you know who she wants to be there and more importantly who to exclude. (Those damn Petersons from down the street, they think they're so special with their prodigy piano playing son who looks like Snoopy...)

**Time to take a Shower**

We have finally got to the nude parts…as if. By shower I am referring to the party that women put together for a woman who is having a woman thing (baby). The word shower has to do with the attention and gifts being showered down on the mommy-to-be. It's cute…so make sure you have a golf game scheduled for that day with your boss so you can't get out of it. Otherwise you will be sucked into attending. Apparently, some sensitive male made a precedence that it's okay for men to attend. Once one guy does it, you can't go back… your stuck. If you can find a pair of tiny earbuds and snake the wire down your back to the FM receiver in your back pocket, you can suffer through the event by listening to College Basketball while nodding and smiling at everyone as yet another pink frilly outfit is pulled from an equally pink frilly box. Remember, when you hear that 3 point shot that ties the game and forcing a double overtime, do not jump up and scream, "Slam it, in your face"… and if you do, just play it off by forcing a little tear and sob and state, I love that thing and point in the general direction of one of the gifts. Women, who don't really understand the dog brained nature of men, will smile, maybe pat you on the shoulder and say to themselves, 'that poor baby'. (To look on the bright side, there will likely be food…)

It is possible that some husbands/boyfriends/significant others including hot lesbian girlfriends may be attending in support. Okay, perhaps the latter is wishful dreaming, but it is likely that there will be some men there. They will be the ones holding babies and carrying diaper bags which suspiciously look like their wives oversized purse. Don't worry; your day is coming when you can look just as pathetic. The things we do for mommies and babies. I am sure that Heaven will have a place for men who did the right thing at the right time…and I am sure that there will be a hot lesbian there too.

## Games of the non-profitable gambling type

You have been included in the shower and it is expected of you to partake in some party games that are both an offense to men everywhere and of questionable intent. The best thing to do is just be prepared for the games and plan on kicking some serious pregnant ass or... hide in the bathroom to catch up on half-time totals.

1) Guess the Tummy Size: (Materials- string or yarn and scissors) Have each woman pull the yarn to the size they believe would fit perfectly around the mommy-to-be's center of her pregnant tummy. After everyone cuts their string, compare the results to the mommy-to-be's actual tummy. Give a prize to the woman who comes closest! This is a baby shower favorite for women. The husband/boyfriend/significant other of the mommy-to-be doesn't get to play. It's too easy to win. Just pretend you're hugging her and measure your arms. Duh.

2) Can't say "Baby": (Materials- baby safety pins or another type of baby object you can place on a string for each woman at the party as well as string or yarn, enough for each woman to wear as a necklace). Have each woman place the necklace with the baby safety pins around her neck when she gets to the party. The rules for this baby shower game are given out at the beginning of the baby shower that whenever someone says the word "baby" during the shower, any woman who calls it out gets a pin from the other woman who stated the word. At the end of the baby shower, the woman with the most pins wins a prize. Men can play a modified version where you cannot say , "Man, look at those hooters", at which point a beer is taken. Of course the beers pass by so often that it gets warm and not worth drinking.

3) Name the Baby Thing: (Materials- pad of paper and pen for each woman). Have each woman write down as many baby products as they can name (bottle, blanket, pacifier, etc) within 5 minutes. Sure it is easy at the beginning, but towards the last few minutes, the women will start racking their brains for more :) Give a prize to the woman who gets the most baby products named!  Unfortunately this isn't played like Scattergories where only the original answers get counted...otherwise your answers of, 'the mouth thing...the pull over the head thing...the smelly thing' and my favorite... 'the boob' would win the game every time.

4) Who Can Make The Mommy-To-Be's Baby: (Materials - baby magazines, Scissors, Glue, Paper). Have the women group up into teams of 3 and give each 3 baby magazines. Have them cut out pieces of different baby qualities and put together a picture of what they think the mommy to be's baby will look like. Have the mommy to be pick which baby would possibly look like hers the best! Give prizes to the winning team! Unless you've picked up scrapbooking and are still carrying around that diaper bag that strangely resembles a woman's purse, you have no chance of winning.  Instead, just cut out any old baby picture and draw arrows to key features and write things like... Eyes as beautiful as her mommy, hair as luxurious as her mommy's, lips as kissable as her mommy's... you get the picture.  Suck up loads and the game is yours.

5) Guess the Baby Food: (Materials - Gerber's infant food, pads of paper and pens). Take the labels off of the baby food jars and have the women at the baby shower guess the food (carrots, peas, sweet potato). Most fun to play up to 10 jars of different kinds of foods. If there is a tie, blindfold the women and have them taste one of the jars and guess the right flavor to win their prize.  Before the

game, preload some of your favorite flavors like Liverwurst, Pickle, Pimento, Nacho Cheese...otherwise, this is a good game to take a break and hide in the bathroom.

6) Guess How Many Safety Pins: (Materials- safety pins and jar). Pass around a jar full of baby safety pins. The one who guesses the closest wins a baby shower prize. It would be worthwhile if you were guessing nuts or hard candy coated chocolates, at least if you won you could put it to use.  Make sure you are not on the team to have to count them first...that is an all night chore that you don't want to have nightmares over... one hundred fifty one, one hundred fifty two, two large boobs, one hundred... what??  Oh, just write down 169.

7) How Well Do You Know Mommy-To-Be: (Materials- pre-printed form and pen for each woman). Have each women guess what features she wants most on the baby from either her or her husband (daddy to be). An example of this idea is found below:

| Attribute | Mommy | Daddy |
|---|---|---|
| Eyes | X | |
| Ears | | X |
| Nose | X | |
| Legs | X | |
| Hair | | X |
| Smile | X | |
| Intelligence | | X |
| Humor | | X |
| Other | X | |

Select 25 attributes and ask everyone to fill in the form from what each woman feels the "Mommy-To-Be's" point of view" will be. After everyone checks off the list, have the mommy to be state her preference. The one with the most correct match to the Mommy-To-Be wins a prize. As everyone is grading themselves like when you were in 7<sup>th</sup> grade, do what you did then. Wait to write down your answer until she gives you the results. I loved 7<sup>th</sup> grade, my parents were so proud.

8) Place The Baby On The Mommy: (Materials- cutouts of a baby with tape and blindfold). Another one of our favorite baby shower games is the baby shower version of Pin The Tail on the Donkey. Blindfold each participant and then give them a paper baby to then approach the mommy to be and place the baby as close to the tummy as possible. The one who gets closest to placing the paper baby on the pregnant tummy wins. Of course if the daddy to be gets anything on the breast, he wins...who cares about the game.

9) Bottle Bong Races: (Materials- baby bottles with Milk or alternate drink). Have each participant take a bottle filled with a liquid and suck the bottle as a baby would. The woman who drinks the most in an allotted time wins the baby shower gift. Might I suggest you pad your own bottle with Pina Colada ahead of time...looks like milk, but will help you make it through the rest of the games with much less stress.

10) Beach Blanket Baby Bingo: (Materials- pens, pre-printed Bingo cards that use the numbers of how many people attend the baby shower) Prior to opening the baby shower gifts, number each gift on the box starting with one. If you know that 15 people will be attending your shower, pre-print bingo cards with numbers 1 through 15 and randomly place them on 15 cards. When the mommy to be decides to open the presents, she grabs the present she wants to open and reads the number out loud. As soon as someone receives bingo, they win the baby shower game and the baby shower prize. I threw in the

beach blanket because by now you are probably tired and could use a nap.

11) "B" is for Baby: (Materials- paper and pens passed out to all the women). Each woman is told to write the baby's mommy to be and daddy to be's name on a paper going vertically down the page. Next to each letter of both names, create a word that is baby related or things that kids like. An example of using the names Kim and Dan:

K= kite      D=drool

I= ice cream    A=alphabet

M= mother     N=nap

The one who guesses the most words that are the same as the mother-to-be wins a prize. My answers for Kim and Dan are as follows: K=Koala because they're warm and fuzzy and bite if you get too close, I=I am so tired of this game that I can't go on, M=Mom, can't you do the rest of this for me... I'm your baby and Dan and I would like to go outside and play ball for a while...

12) Guess the baby item: (Materials- any baby products and blindfold). A bag of baby items are placed in front of the mommy to be for her to take one item out at a time blindfolded and tell her baby shower guests what item she has in her hands. This is really fun baby shower game when you choose some crazy baby toys or products. Just remember, it is not tasteful, especially if your mom is present, to put in the bag certain adult toys.

13) Finish the Baby Rhyme: (Materials- baby rhyme game or a book containing the rhymes). Have the host read out loud a part of the rhyme to be finished by the other women. Let's see how many Baby Shower Guests can finish the following Rhymes we have all grown up with:

1) Mary had a little lamb, it's _____ was white as snow.

2) Baa, baa, black sheep, have you any _____?

3) Mary, Mary, quite _____, how does your garden grow?

4) Rub-a-dub-dub, three men in a tub, and how do you think _____ _____ _____?

5) Pat-a-cake, pat-a-cake, _____ _____!

6) Little Jack Horner, sat in a corner, eating his _____ pie;

7) Little Miss Muffet, sat on a tuffet, eating her _____ and _____.

8) Peter Piper picked a peck of _____ _____.

9) One, two, buckle my shoe, three four, _____ at the door.

10) Peter, Peter, pumpkin-eater, had a wife but couldn't _____ her.

11) Old Mother Hubbard, went to the _____.

12) There was an old woman, who lived in a _____.

13) Jack Sprat could eat no fat, his wife could eat no

_____.

14) Hey diddle, diddle, the _____ and the fiddle.

15) Rock-a-bye baby, on the _____.

Here are the answers below to the questions. It is great to give the winner a baby shower small gift for participating. Read the answers that people have put out loud since you will have some funny ones.

| | | |
|---|---|---|
| 1) fleece | 2) wool | 3) contrary |
| 4) they got there | 5) Baker's man | 6) Christmas |
| 7) curds, whey | 8) pickled peppers | 9) knock |
| 10) keep | 11) cupboard | 12) shoe |
| 13) lean | 14) cat | 15) treetop |

I was out early on because where I grew up, that Mary chick and her  whole family has fleas, so why would I think her sheep would have something different.

14) Guess the baby pictures: Ask for everyone's pictures prior to the baby shower. Have all the pictures in a collage and make lines for people to fill in who they think the babies are out of the girls at the baby shower. If most women don't know each other, just have the pictures of the mother, mother-in-law, sisters, and mommy to be. See how many people guess right. You can make copies of the baby picture collage to see how many can guess right! Or, you could take some random baby photos of people no one knows and play the same game.  It's far more interesting when people believe that the person in the photo is Cousin Marge.

15) Baby Scrambler: Another fun baby shower game is to choose around 25 baby related items and scramble the spelling. For instance, pacifier can be changed to reiifpca. Have the women unscramble the words. The one who gets the most right in 5 min receives a baby shower prize. I just believe this is a cruel game played on the dyslexic.

16) Baby Song List: (Materials - pad of paper and pen for each woman). Have each woman write down in 5 minutes all the songs that have baby in their titles (i.e., Baby Love, Santa Baby, One for My Baby). You can make it harder by stating that you have to name who also wrote the songs! A baby shower favorite! 'Nobody tells baby to stand in the corner', oh, that doesn't count.

17) Pass the Dirty Diaper: (Materials- diaper, chocolate, music player). One of our "dirtiest" baby shower games is for the host to take a diaper that has been "fixed" with warm chocolate in the right place and have the woman pass it to the woman next to them (make sure everyone is in a circle). When the host stops the music, whomever is holding the diaper is out of the game. To make it more interesting, secretly substitute the prop diaper with a real one...loaded of course. Ask Dan, I saw him walking around earlier with a horrible grimace on his face.

18) Place the pacifier in the baby's mouth: (Materials- blindfold, create a baby picture and a few pacifier drawings with one for each woman). Tape a picture or drawing of a baby on the wall and have the blindfolded women try to tape the pacifier as close to the mouth of the baby as possible (The baby shower version of Pin the Tail on the Donkey). Not as much fun as putting paper babies on the Mommy-To-Be.

19) Blindfold Diapering: (Materials- blindfold, baby life size doll(s), diapers). One of the funniest baby shower games is for the women break into teams (up to five persons per team). Each team has a doll, blindfold and diapers. The object is for each participant to place the blindfold on, take the current diaper off the doll and place the new one on while blindfolded. After the first person finishes diapering, they run to the next team-mate who places the blindfold on and has to do the same. The first team to finish diapering wins! Again, a great opportunity to substitute the prop diaper with a real one...this is good when you are trying to get your mother in law to leave.

20) Baby Tic-Tac-Toe: (Materials- Large paper or erasable board to make the tic-tac-toe board, writing utensil, and baby facts). People are broken up in teams and have to answer a question about a baby fact. If they get the answer right, they get to choose a space (like the classic tic-tac-toe game). Of course the questions should not rely on subjective answers...like, 'which bear is best'...'well, there's two schools of thought...' .... 'wrong, black bear is best'

Okay, game time is over. Everyone leaves and you now have more gifts than can fit in your gas saving but very tiny automobile. You then think, 'where is all that going to fit into our equally small house'? You are on your own there. A word of advice; before going to the party, borrow a truck from a buddy. And don't borrow one of those little tiny trucks that looks like a roller skate on steroids. Fet a real man's truck with a minimum 6' bed and which suck an entire tank of gas.

Talking about carrying a load, it's time we talked about what you are going to need to have packed and ready to go before the delivery date. The truck is optional.

## SURVIVAL TIP

**Survival Tip:  Well Wishers and Guests**

You will likely host many friends and relatives that you haven't seen for years, many coming by to say congratulations and to tell you horror stories about birth.  They will all come with sage advice and wisdom that only parenting can provide.  You may not welcome all the extra attention, but for her it will be imperative that people recognize and appreciate the new challenge in her life.  She will need to feel appreciated and respected as a member of the 'continuation of the species' subset of society.  Some may bring gifts and you may feel uncomfortable and wonder if you should be offering them a gift in return.  The answer is no.  Just take the gift, smile, and tell them how thoughtful.  Soon with your own parenting wisdom, you will find that you will be visiting first time parents telling them that if you'd just gotten to them a few months earlier you could have saved them from this fate.  Then laugh sardonically so they don't know if you really meant the statement or not.

**Survival Tip:  How to make an emergency gift box**

Empty a cereal box making sure the inside of the box is not printed.  Carefully pull the bottom portion open, then take a box knife and carefully cut at one of the side creases.  Turn the box inside out and tape the long end.  Fold the end closed and tape it... Viola, a box that can be wrapped for a gift.

## Chapter 10 - How to pack like a man and mean it

The clock is ticking, the time is coming. How and what to pack is now at the forefront of your mind. It's not like packing for a honeymoon where your only concern was shorts ...and that was it, you planned to be naked most of that trip. This time, you are responsible to help define the contents of the bags and getting them to where they need to be.

First and foremost, create a list of what you will need in the bags and which bag things are in. Label your bags clearly. Keep Bag #1 in the trunk of the car you will likely be driving to the hospital, keep bag #2 near the way you intend to leave your house when it's time. Keep a checklist in the car to glance over prior to leaving for the hospital. This should be your visual queue to remember to have both bags, cameras, batteries...

Plan to pack 2 bags, the first for the delivery and the second for the hospital stay after delivery.

### Bag #1 – The "Oh Crap! What do you mean it's time?" Bag

- Focus Item – During delivery classes they told you to bring something for her to focus on to get her mind off the pain of child birth
- Water – She won't be able to drink any unless they decide that labor is going to take a long, long time... otherwise it's ice chips for her. However, she will not want you to leave her side for a second... so bring water.
- Snacks – Same as water
- Slippers – Fuzzy or whatever, the hospital will provide cheap slippers in case you forget, but to help alleviate stress its always better to bring things from home that make her comfortable...and you want her comfortable!

- Robe – She will need something to throw over that horrible hospital gown. Make sure you have a nice clean one and not the one she had hung over the bathroom door that is threads away from being obscene.
- Video Camera – We talked about this…you will want to record as much of the delivery process as possible. Consider using it for reasons such as…why you shouldn't have more children, evidence that you were there, proof that she said horrible hateful things to you for later sympathy points…
- Digital Camera – 95% of the photos you take at the hospital will be useless, still the baby mama will insist, so snap away skippy
- Music, Movies and More… many people believe that having music playing or some other distraction will help them through labor. Not a bad idea, but like most things it only has a small percentage of working. Pack it anyway to prove that you listened and did what you said you would. You may want to consider bringing word games like crossword puzzles or logic problems; these will help keep you and her occupied during some of the down time. Cards are good too, there are many games you can play with a simple deck of cards, including solitaire which you can convince her to play while you catch a few zzzzs. Thinking hard is not going to help the baby come sooner, but it would give her something other than the pain and frustration to focus on.
- List of contact names and numbers…you would like to trust that your or her cell phone will have the key numbers to call once the baby is born… but other than calling your mother and if you can figure out how she listed her mom on her phone, hers, it is not likely you will remember who you wanted to contact. Keep this typed list in the bag. Leave a space at the bottom to write down the name of the hospital, doctor, room number, room phone, baby height and weight and sex if you don't already know it.

When you start making calls, everyone will ask these basic things. It would help if you also knew the baby's name at that point, but if you have been less than diligent at nailing down the name opting for the slacker, 'we'll see who she looks like when she comes out and then decide' attitude, this will at least provide enough information.

- Phone number of florist...after the baby is born, be a man and order your significant other some flowers. You will feel like a jerk when everyone but you bought flowers. Sure, you can do the last minute dash to the hospital gift shop... you can also flush a few extra bucks down the toilet for some crappy flowers. Trust me, go with a florist. You don't need to buy the baby a gift, but it is not a bad idea. If you do, get something small that can be kept in a keepsake box. The baby's mommy will insist on keeping everything from that day including all her firsts...gifts, cards...

- Pen... Take more than one because inevitably one will stop working. You will need this for word games, writing down key information, taking notes....

- A small notepad...these are invaluable, they are good for writing down things she needs, what people said (there is a section in baby books where they ask for first impressions... if you have people on the phone notifying them, you can write down wonderful sentiments like... "OMG you breeders contributed to the overpopulation...", "Sir, this is the pizza palace, while it's great that you just had a baby, we really need to know if you want pan or Sicilian style pizza..."

- A paper bag! When women start breathing exercises, at times they can breathe too fast and hyperventilate. Simply have her breath in and out into a paper bag which will help overcome lightheadedness.

Bag #1 should be kept in the car at least a month early. Make sure to replace snacks and water often so they don't go rancid. It is critical to put a label on the bag.  I would suggest getting some yellow tape and wrap it around the handle, then take a permanent marker and writer her, not your name on it.  She is the patient and the hospital will have a better chance of returning it if they know who she is.

**Bag #2 – The "You forgot to pack…" Bag**
Bag #2 needs to be packed ahead of time and ready to go near the door that you normally use when you leave your house.  If it is getting closer to the delivery day, it won't hurt to keep the bag actually in the trunk along with bag #1.  This should be a normal sized bag and the intent is to provide the mom and baby with the items they will need in the hospital and for the trip home.

- PJs – While your significant other will be far too tired to want something other than the less than appealing hospital gown the first day, by the next day she will be looking for a pair of sweats or at least some comfortable clothes to cover up with.  Some nice large PJs will help out.  Also, you should still have her robe from bag#1 to cover up with
- Unmentionables – She will need a breast feeding bra or at least pads to restrict leakage from her breasts during the first couple of days whether she chooses to breast feed or not.  On their own, her breasts will want to make milk.  Underwear on the first day or so may be unnecessary.  After giving birth she will be fitted with a very large and unattractive belt that holds in place an equally ugly and large pad to catch blood and other leakage from her nether regions.  It makes wearing knickers a disturbing thought, but bring some just in case.
- Comfy clothes for her – She will need to consider the clothes she wore at 6 months and plan to pack those for the hospital and trip home.  This will be the approximate size she will be after delivering the baby.  Just like a takes a little while for a black eye to go down, it will take a while

for her body to recover from delivery. Until then, she needs clothes that won't be restrictive and are comfortable to sit and lay down in. Bring at least a few days worth of clothing as the stay in the hospital may go longer than expected or if the baby or she becomes messy warranting a change in clothes. And don't forget some shoes, she can't leave in her slippers.

- Baby clothes – by now you should know what a onesie is, the t-shirt kind of thing that snaps under the diaper. This is the baby's underwear and will likely be used for up to a year. Bring a few of these as well as a sleeper or layette. A sleeper is a footed soft pajama that goes over the onesie. A layette looks like a bag at the bottom and has an opening for the head and arms at the top. The only thing that makes sense about the design is that you are not struggling to undo the baby's clothes to change a diaper. Bring a few of these. Bibs! Babies barf, therefore they need bibs to catch the barf rolling off their face. Cloth burp rags: these protect your clothes and gives you a little distance from the barf, they are also good to wipe up barf. Lastly, babies lose heat through their head therefore it is important to keep a cap on them, so be sure to bring one of those too.

- Cosmetic and hygiene items – She will want to look pretty for visitors and the baby and may want some makeup to freshen up with. She could also use some deodorant and a toothbrush and toothpaste to keep the funky smells to a minimum. The hospital will provide shower items but if she prefers a certain soap and shampoo you will want to pack those as well. You can find small sized products in the pharmacy as well as travel containers. You should keep liquid items in small sealed plastic baggies to keep them from leaking into other things, nothings worse than your mouthwash sporting an old spice tang. She should help identify what to bring in her cosmetics bag and while this is the list for bag #2, consider this a sub-bag which may or may not fit in bag #2. She should remember things like a brush for her hair and nail clippers...often oversights by women.

- Books, music and videos – she will have some down time to watch television or to talk to people, but that gets old very quick and the newborn babe isn't really that entertaining for the first couple of days. So it's a good idea to give her something to do while she is stuck in a bed. Nothing heavy because she will still be out of sorts from the delivery and the shock that there is something there to take care of that was just a concept a day or two before.

- Do not bring... Cell Phones – Hospitals won't let you have them..., vice items including alcohol and cigarettes. The hospital may allow smoking in certain areas of the hospital, but if there any time to quit smoking this would be it. Other electronics including laptops and gaming systems. They are not an issue with the hospital itself, however expensive items, regardless of how nice a hospital may seem, tend to grow feet and walk away when unattended.

- Your own clothes – you may need to spend the night with her to provide extra support as she will likely feel afraid of the responsibility of the new baby as well as sleeping someplace away from home. Unless you have adopted the attitude of an urban outdoorsman (homeless guys), you may want to consider your own clean up kit including a toothbrush and a change of clothes.

- Stationary items – Bring a notebook with paper and a pen or two to write with, no real reason other than you may be inspired to write down something someone said or begin scheduling out your college savings plan for the baby...or she may start in on you with a 'Honey-do' list and if you don't write it down, those hormones that started nine months ago are still in full swing and could come back to bite you in the rear!

- A large trash bag or two – you will want to bag up soiled garments in one to pack back in the bag before leaving the hospital. Also, people will bring you things in the hospital that you will need to take home with you, what better place to put that hideous floral arrangement that your mole infested great aunt gave you than in a lovely black garbage bag. Just realize that whatever you take in to the hospital you will also need to take out. Make sure you have an empty trunk to contain everything you've brought or acquired during the stay. The baby and his or her new mommy will need to use the back seat for the drive home.

**Tip:** It would be a good idea that when you make some trips home to pick up things you forgot on this very concise list, that you take some of the flowers and gifts visitors left behind home and place them in the nursery. This will make coming home an enjoyable experience.

**Finding True North: The Sun Method**

1. **During the morning**, if you keep the Sun to your right, you will be facing mostly North. This is because, for most latitudes, the Sun rises more toward the East (for both northern and southern hemispheres). This approximation is not accurate or useful at the higher latitudes in the morning and should not be used.
2. **During the hours near "high noon"** (the time when the Sun is highest in the sky for that locality), face away from the Sun to head mostly North for most northern latitudes or face toward the Sun for most southern latitudes. This is because the Sun is exactly North or

South at high noon. For those latitudes within about 23 degrees of the equator, the Sun may be either North or South at high noon depending on the day of the year. This approximation is not accurate or useful at those latitudes which are close to the equator for some parts of the year and should not be used since the Sun will be almost directly overhead near high noon.

3. **During the evening**, if you keep the Sun to your left, you will be facing mostly North. This is because, for most latitudes, the Sun sets more toward the West (for both northern and southern hemispheres). This approximation is not accurate or useful at the higher latitudes in the evening and should not be used.

**Shadow-Tip Method**

1. Place a stick securely in the ground so that you can see its shadow. The stick does not need to be straight or at any particular angle relative to the ground. Alternatively, you can use the shadow of any fixed object. Nearly any object will work, but the taller the object is, the easier it will be to see the movement of its shadow, and the narrower the tip of the object is, the more accurate the reading will be. Make sure the shadow is cast onto a level, brush-free spot.
2. Mark the tip of the shadow with a small object, such as a pebble, or a distinct scratch in the ground. Try to make the mark as small as possible so as to pinpoint the shadow's tip, but make sure you can identify the mark later.
3. Wait 10-15 minutes. The shadow will move mostly from west to east in an arc which depends on your latitude, season and time of day.
4. Mark the new position of the shadow's tip with another small object or scratch. It will likely move only a short distance.

5. Draw a straight line in the ground through the two marks. This is approximately an east-to-west line.
6. Stand with the first mark (west) on your left, and the other (east) on your right. You are now facing approximately toward true north. (Accuracy improves as your location approaches the equator, as the time of year approaches either equinox and as the time of day approaches midday.)

**The Cow Method**

If you are near a field with cows and notice that some are resting or lying down, the direction a cow lays to rest is typically with its head pointing north.

**Part II – "It's time, what?  What do you mean?? OMG!.. Where's my keys, the bag, did you remember that thing you knew I'd forget?  How do we get to the hospital?  WTF, I need to call my mom…." – This is a very important chapter about the time you've been ~~dreading~~ looking forward to.**

**Chapter 1 – False Positive is just as much an oxymoron as False Labor**

Anxiety, anxiousness and ants in your pants are just a few of the feelings as you enter the ninth month of pregnancy.  The doctor or midwife has told her to start coming in weekly for measurements and to check the baby out.  This can be a very stressful time for you, the mom and the baby.  Your nerves will be worn thin as you start playing through your mind all the things you were supposed to do, all the plans you made ahead of time and the inevitability that your life will never be the same in just a few short weeks. The last thing on your mind is relaxing. So comes the false labor.

As a woman's body prepares to deliver, many things are happening inside of her. The baby is getting into position to leave the body and if all is right, it should be head down facing the mommy's back. It will continue to drop lower toward the exit from wenst the seed came, kind of like a Jack Kerouac journey in search of his origin. The top of the uterus (womb) is called the Fundus which is where contractions normally start. However, she may experience feelings that very closely resemble contractions called Braxton Hicks.

Braxton Hicks contractions act and feel like the real thing, however, they do not cause the cervix to dilate, and if the cervix doesn't dilate, no baby is coming. Try to tell her they are fake and expect to be backhanded as there is no possible way you can know what a contraction feels like. If it is her first, technically, there is no way for her to know either. She may realize that it is false labor and smack you anyway because by using the word "fake" or "false" does not lessen the pain she is experiencing. Some doctors like to call false labor "tremors before the big quake." There are a few key things to do if she thinks she is having contractions:

1.  Time the contractions. Mark the time the contraction starts and mark again when the next contraction starts. Use this as you guide. Mark the next set and the set after to see if they are consistent. If they are close and consistent, it could be real labor. You may need to do this several times, and with real labor over time the contractions will get closer together. If it is the first baby, you can expect labor to last around 12 hours, so there is time to continue to measure the labor pains. However, if the contractions are occurring every 3 to 5 minutes, get to

the hospital; you don't want to deliver the baby yourself in the car.

2. Have her drink some water.  Believe it or not, sometimes false labor is triggered by dehydration.  By hydrating, if the contractions lessen, become further apart or just go away...viola, false labor has been positively identified.
3. Change positions.  Real labor won't care if you are laying, sitting, walking, turning or whatever, the pain just continues to come.  If the pain stops or lessens by changing positions, it is very likely false labor.
4. Take a warm shower or rest, again if the pain goes away then you are out of the woods
5. If the pain is felt from the belly to the groin, it is likely false labor.  True labor is felt from the back to the belly giving a wrap around feeling.
6. If the water breaks...leave, it is not false labor, it is the real thing and you should stop reading this book and call your doctor and midwife and tell them how far apart the contractions are and describe the Color, Odor, Amount of and Time the water broke. (It's easy to remember by its initials:  COAT, or if you are hungry TACO)  The hospital will want to know as much detail regarding TACO that you can tell them.
7. Never stop counting the time as long as the false labor is active, if the contractions continue consult your midwife or doctor.

Does it hurt to make a trip to the hospital just to be sure.  As guys we would say that it is a waste of time.  That stays in this book by the way, but it would be wise to talk to the midwife or doctor over the phone to ease her mind.  False labor can happen many times and like the boy that cried wolf, you may fall into a false sense of urgency.  Just remember, sooner or later, the labor pains will be real and it will be time to go, so you can never assume. The best thing to do now is to recap this short chapter. Unfortunately the next few chapters are long.  You can use that to your advantage as a comparable when the baby mama starts talking about how long she was in labor...you spent an incredible amount of time reading these longer chapters. That doesn't mean that the information contained within these hallowed bindings are not valuable.

Summary of Chapter One – False Labor

A. Time the labor to determine if they are getting closer and are consistent
B. Have her change positions, shower or rest
C. Drink Water
D. Call Doctor or Midwife if pain continues

## Chapter 2 – Time to get real...get to the hospital real fast

So, you say she's having a baby. That may be, and you've done what you could to make sure it was for real this time, you've got the bump on your head from the glass juicer she threw at you for questioning her sincerity. After confirmation that it is time, whether you or she is ready to go you are on your way.
Let's step back for a minute. When should you leave for the hospital? A first time mom will tell you as soon as the contractions start, that is why you went home three times with false labor. Those cute movies at the child birthing classes told you that you have time to take it easy and sleep through the early stages of labor. Please! A first time mom experiencing what she believes is actual labor... there is no sleep for you nor her. Anxiety levels are high, adrenaline is through the roof and all the education and training which made you both agree that you wouldn't be "those" people who panicked are indeed, "those" people.

**SURVIVAL TIP**

**Survival Tip: Overcoming False Labor**

Never assume that labor is false. If the labor pains are more than five minutes apart, you have time to check if the labor is true or false. She should try to rest, take a warm shower, drink water and move around. If the pains stop, she is not in labor. If they continue, you need to keep checking the time between contractions. If they continue and get closer and more painful, call the doctor or midwife. Don't wait. See the section in the book on Real Labor to know what to do it you are wrong.

**Survival Tip: Catch a speeding baseball or other object hurled at you incredibly fast**

Babies can pop out quickly once the shoulders clear the cervix and midwives and doctors are adept at catching them. Without a glove, catching a speeding baseball can prove to be painful or injurious. Why someone is throwing a baseball, rock or other object at you is up to your own inventive imagination. Perhaps it's a butter dish from your mother that the pregnant mommy is throwing at you for stating that her labor is false and to just ignore it and it will go away. Either way, this may take some practice, but you should learn how to do a matching speed catch. Extend your arm out with your hand open, turn your shoulder into the direction of the object, spread your feet should width apart. Think of the object like catching a Frisbee and match the speed with your hand drawing back your arm and shoulder, make sure you grasp the object and begin to spin around following the direction of the ball. After one revolution the inertia of the ball should be slowed enough to stop without injury or pain. This takes incredible hand eye coordination, timing and practice, but it could save your head and marriage ;)

This segment is over but I thought you would appreciate some very cool car images:

1967 Pontiac GTO

How do you determine that the labor pain is real? Shouldn't your body just know? After all, your ancient relatives who carried clubs and lived in caves had babies, hence you. (Less the major monobrow thing, and if not you should seriously consider tweezing because you are scaring small children). Still, nature allows all other animals on earth to give birth just by knowing.

**Here are some signs that labor is coming soon:**

Nesting – She will start cleaning and organizing. She will be all over you about not finishing those chores you had nine months to complete. Not every woman nests, and some do it in varying degrees from mild to … well building an actual nest.

The Baby Drops – not out of her, but it drops lower in her body so that the head is in the pelvis area between her hip bones. This is also known as lightening, but if you had something in your gut right there, it definitely isn't light. Yes, you should probably discontinue sex now, you don't want to live with those memories 20 years later. Also, a little known fact is that nipple stimulation during this time could bring on very strong and fast labor.

False Labor – Many people believe that False labor is the rehearsal before the real thing.

She suddenly has energy – All of a sudden its like she is not even pregnant. She wants to go out shopping, doing household chores… it's a farce and it is also getting close. The body is getting ready to give her a burst of energy to deal with the baby that is on its way.

The baby moves less – Like carb loading before a big game or big race, many people believe the reason the baby stops moving as much the day before delivery is to conserve energy for the big event.

<u>The Poo is ... well, I wouldn't check it but ask her</u> – she may experience very loose stool and diarrhea shortly before labor as the baby is pushing all the urine and fecal matter out, it needs all the room in that area it can get.

**Here are some signs that labor is for real:**

<u>Labor Pain</u> – This should be obvious, but when faced with other false labor episodes, it is hard to say if the labor is real. The plain and simple test is to time the labor contractions and go through the motions that you would for false labor. If the pain is consistent and increasing, and doesn't go away with the false labor methods, it's probably for real.

Bloody Show – And no this is not the all night sci-fi Vampires from Space movie you were waiting to come out on the big screen... this refers to a bloody discharge that comes out of the cervix as the space loosens and begins to open. When she first got pregnant, this mucus barrier was formed to keep infection out. Many people freak out when they see it, some even believe that it's the baby and wonder why it looks so messy (seriously, some people actually wonder). Think of it like bloody snot, just not typically as red.

Water Breaks – you can make fun of her all you want, but she didn't pee herself...at least not this time. Some women experience their water breaking while they are in labor. Normally it's a leakage, but it is important to collect some data:

Color – describe the color of the fluid (yellowish, greenish, brownish, reddish, clear...)

Odor – Does it smell like urine, is it strong and foul, is it smelly like the fish market...

Amount – How much came out, was it a gush, was it a trickle, could you fill up a glass, two, a bucket

Time – When did it break

The acronym is COAT (or TACO if you are hungry) and it is important to get this information to the doctor or midwife to make sure everything is okay. There are some serious conditions that could arise based on your answers. Definitely call as soon as her water breaks. Just be prepared that they may tell you to wait at home until the contractions are 5 minutes apart, also be prepared that you might need to **call 911 immediately if the cord pops out.**

**The baby is crowning** – Okay, if you got this far without believing that labor is real, she should have checked you on the other side of the head with that juicer glass. If the head starts to appear coming out of her vagina, do not panic. Tell her to breath and not to push. **Call 911**.

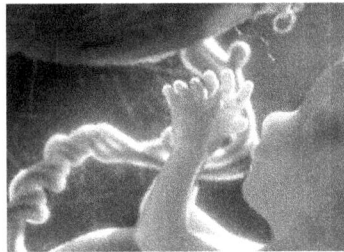

Back to the timeline... You should have measured the contractions which progressed to the point that they were occurring every 3 to 5 minutes. This is when you should be quickly on your way to the hospital. The midwife or physician will tell you by phone to come in.

So you are in your car, her delivery bag is in the back seat and the overnight bag is in the trunk. She will experience pains during the drive and will not want to put the seat belt across the lap. It is best to have her sit in the back seat where she can stretch out and in the event of an accident will not be hit with the airbag. She should still at least put a shoulder strap across the chest. Your job is to drive safe and alert. There is still plenty of time. The doctor/midwife told you it was okay to come to the hospital. Not to call an ambulance and get there with the lights flashing and siren screaming. Police officers may be reluctant to give you a ticket as they don't want to deliver your baby, but that doesn't mean they will give you an escort to the hospital either. There are a couple of things you need to prepare before the imminent date:

- Keep the fuel tank full, you don't want to worry about filling up on the way
- Check your spare and be familiar with how to change it quickly, if you are unsure … practice!
- Make sure you have a clear planned route to the hospital
- Plan an alternate route in the event of traffic or weather issues
- Avoid using your cell phone, if necessary she can still talk on the phone, she shouldn't be unconscious or so incapacitated that she can't yap with one of her girlfriends. But with the amount of pressure to get yourself and her there in one piece, you do not need another distraction
- Bring a cell phone. Don't be silly, don't leave it at home because you need to avoid using it. If something happens you need communication. I told you already not to pack one, but you can at least leave it in your car. For that matter, make sure you have a car adapter to plug the phone into in case you didn't have the time to charge it up before leaving.
- Keep her calm and relaxed. Never let her see you sweat! She needs you to help her count and breath and be the calming voice during the drive. She may be freaking out

and starting in on you and how you planted that seed, she will claim pregnesia later (a form of amnesia associated with pregnancy to help women forget what a horrible experience having a baby is... guys don't have this denial gene)

Did you forget anything?  Probably, but as long as she is in the car and you know how to get to the hospital, everything else can catch up later.  In laws are great resources for running to the house and picking up things.  It is likely the only time you can have your mother in law at your beckoned call.

**IMPORTANT NOTE:**  Make sure at least a month before the delivery that you pre-register at the hospital.  That means that all the patient information, insurance information, patient medical history (and the mountain of other forms) are already done by the time she is in labor.  If you make her sit in the lobby, of if you are stuck in the lobby while she is wheeled away from you, you can expect that she will yank out the juicer glass one more time, and this time it will probably break.

The first tough decision as a soon to be father is to figure out the better of two evils.  Parking.  Should you drop her at the door and make her wait for you to park and run up with the bags.  Should you park the car and make her walk to the door.  In the first scenario, she may feel abandoned and others will look at you like a creep leaving his wife in obvious agony.  Of course, she will give you hell for making her walk the back 9 of the parking lot.  If your hospital does not have valet parking, it should.  Most hospitals won't let you  park in front of the doors and run in.  So, the choice should be made prior to showing up at the hospital. She will likely go for the first option and can meet you in the lobby, preferably in a soft chair. *You can avoid this issue if you plan to have your parents or her parents just meet you there (before you get there) to hand her off to so she won't be alone while you park*.

See, this book was worth the money. That little idea not only saved your marriage, but made your IQ jump 10 points in her eyes. One more like that and you could achieve the ever elusive spousal 100 IQ rating.

## At the Hospital

When a woman comes into the hospital complaining of labor pains she is normally examined by a doctor to determine if she is ready to be admitted or if she needs to go home and wait a while. What did you say? A woman having her first baby averages 16 hours of labor and the hospital is no place to hang out for all that time. To help the labor progress at a good pace, it is often advised by the caregiver to stay at home until she the contractions are coming 3 to 5 minutes apart. Of course it is important for her to stay in contact with the doctor or midwife to determine when it is best to come in.

The physician who checks her to make the determination if she stays or goes will use fancy words like, "Station", "Effaced" and "Dilated". These are pretty important words to understand as they are like the countdown clock on the scoreboard and in a close game, the winner is decided by who makes the last basket.

*Dilation* – if you've heard nothing else through the months of pregnancy, you have probably heard the word dilated or dilation referring to the opening of the cervix that the baby will pass through. What is hard to get your mind around are the numbers. Doctors like to speak in Metric. Like they all went to school in Europe and left socialized medicine to come to America where the money really is at. So when they talk about how big around that hole needs to be, they are speaking in centimeters. I prefer a visual: A dime is a little more than 1 centimeter. A nickel is 2cm, a quarter is 2.5cm. See, it's not so hard. A golf ball is 3.5cm, a tennis ball is 6.5cm. A regulation baseball is about 7.5cm and a

softball is a little larger than 10cm.  10cm is the magic number, but don't worry it's not your job to figure out how big the hole is.
*Effacement* – The cervix needs to thin out and become soft to allow the baby to pass through. This is measured in how firm and thick or soft and thinned out the opening becomes.  This is measured in percentages, sort of like times at bat.  The cervix needs to get to 100% before it is thinned and softened enough for the baby to pass.  If you were to feel the cervix at that moment, it would feel like the soft inside of your cheek.  Make a muscle with your bicep and hold it.  With your other hand feel how firm (and massive) it is.  Next, feel how soft the inside of your elbow is. That is the path the cervix needs to take so it is understandable why it can take 16 hours to get to that point.
*Station* – Stations are measured from -4 to +4 and to the layman it doesn't sound like anything to do with trains or space.  The station is the position of the baby's head in relation to a specific bone in the woman's pelvis.  The baby's head needs to move down into the pelvic bone to start pushing out the softened cervix and past the big hole.  The caregiver must have very calibrated hands to figure out where exactly the head is in relation to the ischial spines of the pelvic bone.  If you were to load a shotgun, you would pull back the bolt to allow the shell into the chamber. This would be -4 station.  If you slowly push forward the bolt, it would move to the point where the business end of the shell enters the chamber end of the barrel.  This is 0 station.  When the shell is pushed all the way in and the bolt is locked into place, you are at +4 station and ready to shoot out that baby.


A woman should not attempt to push until all the prerequisites have been met.  Again, it is not your job to determine where she is at or when it's time to go, you are the score keeper keeping track of the shot clock.  Remember:  10cm, 100% effaced and +4 station means that the baby is on its way out.

## 16 hours of average hell...

The triage area of the hospital has said it is okay to pass, her labor is in full force, perhaps her water has broken,
whatever the reason she is allowed to enter into the sacred birthing room... and wait. If all went according to plan, she probably has been in labor 10 hours to this point. She should be in what is called "Active" labor, which means that those labor pains that she didn't think were so bad, all of a sudden became bad, and the person who said they were going to have the baby completely natural and would refuse any drugs is now pushing the call button and screaming down the hall for an anesthesiologist to start an epidural. Her water may or may break. If it doesn't break on its own, at some point during "active" labor it will be punctured by the caregiver to allow the baby to move down. She may want to start pushing, but as identified earlier when talking about stations and the analogy with a shotgun, if you release the hammer on the shotgun before the bolt is locked into place, the aftermath can be rather messy. To keep from pushing, and to cope with the contractions which are now coming more frequently and with much more force, she will need to practice mind over matter, breathing in and out and transindental meditation.

One minute she will be hot, then cold, will want to be touched...but then, by anybody but you. She will freak out, become focused, become a spaz and rip you a new one, then cry into your collar and tell you how much she loves you. Kind of like your first drunk date. This is where you have one job... **keep her distracted**! She needs to get past the 1 to 3 minute contractions without pushing. She will be in pain and there is nothing either of you can do. For whatever reason, the human body wants to be up and moving during this time and walking not only helps the labor progress, but it lessens the pains to a small degree. Sometimes bouncing on a ball, sitting in a warm shower or bath or listening to nature sounds while blowing rhythmically through the contractions help.  There is no one answer to what will work, and sometimes to keep her distracted you will need to pull out the full arsenal of distraction tactics.

Real hell begins when she has been in "Active", otherwise known as "I will rip your lips off if you say 'I understand sweetie, shhhh, there now it will be alright' ", labor and you ask the caregiver to check her out to see if it's time yet.  Remember, 10cm, 100%, +4.  The sweet midwife walks in and tells her how beautiful she looks and how wonderful the experience is.  You look dumbfounded as she agrees with the midwife.  Apparently the brain is releasing drugs into her sense of perception because when you look at her, she is red, her hair is a mess and it looks like she's been working transmissions at a monster truck mud bogging competition...in July.  The midwife should get an Oscar for her performance, if it were that easy to get her calmed down, they should have taught men that trick before coming to the hospital.  Alas, the chemical that is fooling the woman's mind is sex specific... men don't trigger the same altered perception.  So the midwife reaches up and smiles and nods her head... hurray you scream inside... I'm almost done.  Oh, and so is she.  Pulling her hand out and in one sweep removing the latex glove, popping the biological hazard waste can lid with her foot to discard the limp prophylactic and holding a sardonic smile, she states, "That is very good work sweetheart, we are at 4cm, and 75% effaced.  Just a little more to go", and patting her on the arm she extricates herself from the room before it sinks in and now the soon to be baby mama starts crying.

"Like hell",  you say to yourself because you don't want to seem like an ass in the middle of a hospital with a bunch of women giving birth.  Still, you are incredulous as you are left to deal with the aftermath.  You've expended the full arsenal of tricks to keep her distracted and knowing that you have a long way to go before she is ready....  The prospects don't look good.  You look at your watch, 12 hours.  The last two seemed like ten, surely the sun had risen again and an entire day passed. It cannot be 2 hours, it must be twelve. Listening to your digital watch you realize that you are now making eye contact with a teary bleary eyed mom-to-be with a woeful plea in her eyes like that of a horse with a broken leg wanting to be put down. Okay, not quite like that... and I could never shoot a horse (unless he shot at me first), still, she is in agony.

**It's time to call in the big guns.**

Robert Frost spoke of roads diverging in a yellow wood, one well worn and the other less traveled. I am not sure why the woods were yellow, still, this is a point where people need to make a decision: whether or not to use pharmaceuticals to improve the delivery process or to relieve the pains of labor through more natural methods. Some statistics will tell you that women who have the option to use an epidural prior to labor but decide to go the natural route, will change their minds during active labor at a rate of 60%. Does that mean that women are weak and can't follow through with what nature has managed for the entire existence of man? If it were up to men, 100% of us would elect for an epidural rather than enduring the pain of labor. It is confusing to understand why a woman would want to undergo labor without anything.

Those who do choose the path of pain relief have quite a few options, although you should be aware of any and all adverse effects of taking them. Some allow the woman to sleep to get much needed rest. Some take the edge off so the pain is still there but not as severe. Other techniques fool the brain into believing there is no pain and others cut off the pain receptors to those places where... it hurts!

The drugs and treatments were probably explained before, and will likely be given as options again at the time of delivery. Your job is to remember that some can help her sleep, however they will also make the baby drowsy. This is one type of drug that many women choose to stay away from. You must also know to ask for the drugs that will help lessen the pain. There are a few options here that include non-pharmacological choices. Some just take the edge off while others help with rest and relieving a good portion of pain. If she is in back labor, four small injections on the back of saline through a syringe can help fool the mind into believing the pain is not present without any chemicals. Most of these will allow the woman full activity and full participation in the delivery.

And then there is the epidural. While this has been common practice for decades performed by specialized anesthesiologists, many women are still leery of the adverse affects from sticking a needle into the spine. The risk to the child is very small as it is argued that it would take a long exposure of an epidural to filter into the blood stream and then through the umbilical cord, still any risks should be considered. Also, any time there is a procedure that has to do with the spine, there is a risk of paralysis. It is important to know ahead of time who would be performing the procedure and what experience they have as well as any lawsuits for malpractice on record. It is better to be rude than sorry. With epidurals today, the pain is removed and the woman needs to remain in bed, but unlike epidurals of the past, she can still push with contractions with great affectivity. If she is still on the boundary of decision, she should also consider that if the natural delivery needs to turn into a cesarean section she will receive an epidural whether she chooses one or not. If men had babies, we would call ahead to the hospital to have the anesthesiologist waiting with the epidural in hand. If there is no need for pain, why or why would you welcome it. Just one way men are still the saner sex.

Other side effects of medications could include prolonging labor and after a day and a half, no one wants to prolong labor. There are medicines that can help women move forward through labor if they are failing to progress. Like other medications, these too have side effects. To understand your risk, ask your caregiver prior to coming to the hospital what the options are and the inherit risks.


**Locked and loaded, fire at will**


At last, the prerequisites have been met. She is at 10cm, 100% effaced and +4 station. If you look down there at this point you should see the baby's head crowning (the top of the baby's head is coming through). This part of labor is not for the squeamish. You have the option to stay up by the mommy's head and stay completely oblivious of the miracle of nature...and for most men that is just fine. We don't need to see how hot dogs are made, because if we did we would never yell to the concessionaire to throw one at you in the nose bleed section at the ball park. Because she has been instructed to push, this new phase of labor is called 'delivery', with an obvious outcome.

So the caregiver takes a seat at the business end of the woman, and begins to feel and rub lotion all over her private parts. When a contraction starts she will instruct her to push down and out. There is no direct correlation for men to demonstrate what needs to happen. It is one of the remaining mysteries only ever experienced by the fairer half. What is going on is that the uterus is contracting from the top to help push the baby down and with the mom's support and additional pushing it makes the process even more effective. Neither one can do it alone. When the contractions end the baby that was being pushed out starts to retreat, and if you are keeping score it's like pushing to the line of scrimmage only to be knocked back before being tackled. This is the two steps forward one step back frustrating agony of delivery. It can take from 30 minutes to hours of this game before the baby will make it out. The mother will go through this most exhausting phase using every muscle in her body to get the momentum going.

Your job during delivery is to hold whatever the caregiver tells you to, an arm, a foot, a hand... and encourage her to push and rest when its time. You probably won't be very good, after all no man is a doula. What is a doula you ask? The answer to a man trying to be the birthing coach but knows that he sucks at it. A doula is a professional birthing support person. They come in to help keep the woman focused on the delivery process, to help understand what is happening, to cope with the pains and to give encouragement. Through experience and education, they are better prepared to deal with what is happening. While this is a service you will have to pay for out of pocket, for some dads who are not at all comfortable with the coaching responsibility, it is a good option to consider. For those who don't have the means or for those who want to do it themselves, doula or not, the baby will come regardless.

One of the best functions you can have during the delivery portion is to count down the contraction. You will see the monitor start to peak as she begins to push and you will slowly count down from 30 which is as long as the contraction should last. If it goes longer, count slower. This helps her focus on an end to the pain and effort and helps her tremendously when dealing with the task at hand.

During delivery you may see the caregiver pull out some strange looking torture devices: one that looks like a penis enlarger and the other like shiny tongs to flip steaks over on a grill. These are not used during every pregnancy, but there are times when pushing is just not enough and the caregiver needs to pull the baby while she pushes down on the baby. The first device is a vacuum (yes, it looks a lot like a penis enlarger). It attaches to the crowning head of the baby and sucks on to get a grip. It is then pulled slowly to help guide and direct the baby out. The other is what doctors lovingly call, forceps which strangely resembles the word foreskin and many would fear this if they are having a son... what if the doctor grabs in the wrong place! The device is designed to surround the baby's head and again used to turn and pull the baby out.

**SURVIVAL TIP**

## Survival Tip: Avoiding an Episiotomy

In Europe far fewer women than in the US require an episiotomy (a surgical cut to enlarge the birthing canal) or have tears. This is because they use midwives for the most part and do not force the pushing process. By slowing things down and using some oils, the baby's head will very often push through the vagina without a tear or cut.

## Survival Tip:  Every Man Should know how to:

1. Handle a blowout
2. Drive in snow
3. Jump start a car
4. Replace fan belt
5. Wax a car
6. Perform CPR
7. Perform the Heimlich
8. Treat a snakebite
9. Cast a line
10. Sew on a Button
11. Fix a toilet tank flapper
12. Change a single pole switch
13. Escape a sinking car
14. Carve a turkey
15. Read a map
16. Wire audio visual equipment
17. Polish shoes
18. Use a hammer, screwdriver and wrench
19. Move heavy stuff
20. Grow food
21. Build a fire in the wilderness
22. Build a shelter
23. Find potable water
24. Put out a fire
25. Change a diaper

Especially when using the last device, there sometimes is simply not enough room to get the baby past the mothers' vagina. While many experienced midwives are successful at avoiding this, there may be a need to allow the woman to tear or to cut the perineum. That is the space between the vagina and anus. It is not pretty and you shouldn't watch, but a precise cut or tear will allow enough room to get the head and forceps if used out.

Through all the pushing and pulling, the sweat and pain, when all is said and done, if all goes well, an ugly sticky funny looking thing pops out and someone invariably yells, 'congratulations'. The baby is suctioned, wiped quickly and often put on the mothers chest. A long umbilical cord is still attached which looks more alien than human and will need to be severed. Clamps will be placed on two sides allowing scissors to cut between them thereby separating the baby from the womb forever. NOTE: if the clamps aren't in place, blood would stream from both ends if cut...not good. In some cases the doctor will ask if you want to cut the cord, a ceremonial right of men to partake in something totally gross...almost makes the whole experience worth it. It is a slippery little booger and you need to be careful when holding the scissors.

The baby will need to be placed on a warming table to get suctioned or cleaned up some more and to have some extra tests done. This is not an uncommon procedure as the first few minutes of life are critical. Many times though the baby can lay on the mothers chest and start breastfeeding immediately if desired. It is said that babies that have direct skin contact immediately after birth take the transition of birth easier, sleep better and tend to be calmer. So, it is worth noting.

The next thing to happen is really something men shouldn't be exposed to, but here are the gory details: the placenta needs to be delivered. That is the sack that the baby has been living in the entire term of their pregnancy. It appears to be alien in nature with red and blue veins running over the surface and covered in blood. This thing is not only gross, but could cause you to lose your lunch. The caregiver will "deliver" it a few minutes after the baby comes out which means the mother will need to push one last time, but it will be easy as the baby left a huge hole in its wake. It will be inspected to make sure it's complete. If it is not, it could cause infections and other problems for the mother later on. The blood and tissue are valuable as they contain specialized cells that are used in research and could save lives. Still in the early stages, there is evidence that storing the cord blood by special blood collection agencies could be used to help you or a sibling of the child with some common diseases. There is a cost to the service so do some research, but the benefits if used far outweigh the upfront cost of storage.

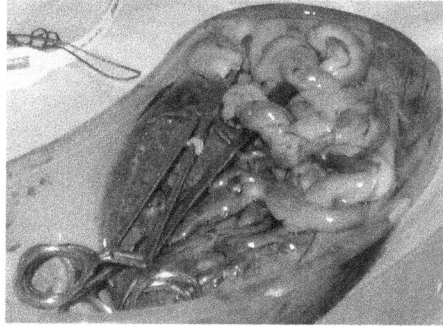

**Now that baby is here**

As you stand in delivery, your woman is bare breasted (funny you didn't notice that before) and she pulls the baby up to her breast to feed. It is very common now for women to attempt to breast feed and is considered the best nutritional source for babies. Within the first hours after birth the mother will produce a highly concentrated liquid (colostrum) from her breasts that will give the baby special powers (or at least some protection) which will keep them from getting certain illnesses through the age of 16. From just one small suckle from the breast, it's more amazing than can be imagined.

You will likely check out all the baby parts to make sure everything is there, toes, fingers, eyes & nose...but there is one appendage you didn't count on. There is something growing out of the belly button with a clamp on the end. This is the connection the baby had to the placenta and in a week or two it will dry out and fall off leaving your baby a lovely little belly button. Your job is to make sure it stays clean and dry so it doesn't get infected.

You may also notice that your baby's privates are much larger than you expected for a baby. This is common as the baby has taken in a lot of its mother's hormones causing those areas to swell. In a day or two they will go back to normal.

Finally, don't worry if the baby opens its eyes and doesn't see you as being familiar. The fact is that the baby can barely see at all, they will see shapes and light and dark and it will take some time before it learns recognition of its daddy. It will come though, and when they are asking for allowance and the car, you will wish it hadn't.

**If you got them, flaunt them**

Once settled in a room it is possible that the new mommy will be all smiles and excited and ready to have another baby. Pregnesia, as it is sometimes referred, is a side affect to the chemicals that the brain sends out after a baby is born to help the mom forget how terrible the delivery actually was. The things most conveniently forgotten are the harsh statements she made about you just shy of ripping your lips off during those difficult contractions. She will probably get weepy, grumpy and sleepy...and dopey and bashful and the rest of the gang before the brain drugs stop affecting her.

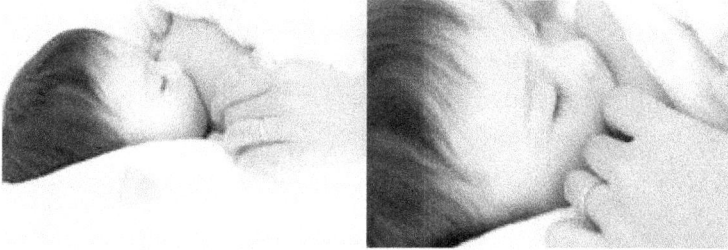

In the meantime baby has probably joined mom for couplet care. (Couplet care is the new hippie idea that babies shouldn't be left in the nursery, they should be with the mom...who mind you just delivered the baby and is otherwise wiped out. Seems like a way for hospitals to reduce staff),  Hospitals are reluctant to keep the babies in nurseries and encourage new moms to take their babies from the hour after the birth.  It has been studied and theorized that babies joined with their mothers shortly after birth tend to have less stress, cry less and have more sound sleep than 20 years ago when they were locked behind glass windows.  It is usually the mom's choice to send the baby to nursery for short spurts during showers or if the mom needs some sleep, and the hospital won't fault the mom if that is the case, but they will encourage couplet care...strongly.

So, back to the **boobs**...if she has chosen to flash you prior to feeding the baby (meaning that she has opted to breast over bottle feed), she will find it will make for a happy, healthy and well adjusted baby.  Studies show that babies who breast feed have a higher IQ on average of 10 points more than bottle fed babies.  They also sleep better, throw up less, have less waste, are sick less, sleep through the night sooner and bond with the mother much sooner.  Also many times the mother returns to her pre-pregnancy weight sooner.  That is all the upside.  The downside is that her boobs will leak.  They may get a little crusty at the nipples, and won't be as much a fun bag as something you want to avoid manhandling too much during intimate moments. Like everything, it will pass and the baby will stop breast feeding and they will be yours again.  You can expect that breast feeding will last up to a year, and is recommended for at least the first 9 months.  One thing you should have packed in the hospital stay bag are some breast pads as she will leak and will need something to keep milk from coming through her shirt...that is unless you are going to a wet t-shirt contest, then by all means provide your own fluids.

## Chapter 3 - When things go wrong

This is not my favorite part to talk about and by no means will I make light of this segment.  It is possible and can be disturbing the things that can go wrong with having babies.  You job is to plan for the worst, to pull on some thick steel skin and be prepared to man up if the need should arise.

**C-section births**.  It is now more common place for women to go in for a cesarean delivery for every reason under the sun including laziness, fear of work or fear of what it will do to the nether regions.  But there are some very valid reasons for a c-section including distress of the baby, a threat to the life  of the baby and/or mother and an inability to pass the baby through the mothers hips... a hundred years ago women and sometimes babies just died.  We are fortunate that today's doctors are prepared and capable of performing such a surgery.  But they are not without risk.  The mother must be sedated with anesthesia which could have adverse side effects.  There is an incision to external and internal body parts which could also get ugly.  Infections, blood loss, contamination, a poor surgeon could all lead to bad results when an invasive procedure is done.  It is always best to attempt to do what nature designed, it may be hard, long and painful...but it is what the female of our species were designed to do.  There are so many coping abilities built into

126

a woman to deal with it, to the point that they are willing to get pregnant more than once.

**Injury**. Although uncommon, it is possible that preeclampsia (pregnancy induced high blood pressure) could cause a stroke. It is also possible that other challenges during delivery could leave a woman debilitated, after all the process is extremely grueling and requires energy, strength and a healthy body. If any of these areas are lacking, injury could occur. Football players perform strength training exercises not to build up their muscles, but to toughen their bodies so they can take the amount of force they face when being hit head on by a running 250 pound man. If they don't work out hard, the likeliness of injury increases.

**Premature labor**. Sometimes trauma or other unexplained event will trigger a premature labor. By 32 weeks a baby is developed enough that if delivered would be small but should be able to breath and function on its own. Before that, there could be some lung issues and other complications usually resulting in a very long hospital stay or even the passing of the infant. Preemies are usually very tiny and will have numerous issues health wise that could follow them for a large portion of their life. The only defense to avoid premature labor is to be careful throughout the pregnancy and notify the doctor if she is experiences labor pains far too soon. There are many times that labor can be stopped and the baby allowed to incubate.

**Physical and mental deformities**. There are a number of conditions that can be tested for prior to delivery in order to identify a physical deformity in the baby. Many parents opt not to know until the baby is born as the options are either to know and worry throughout the pregnancy, because like anything the tests could be wrong, or to abort the baby. If parents will not pursue the abortion, the worry is not worth the stress. Still, some babies are born with all sorts of deformities from dwarfism to Downs syndrome, to conjoined twins and so on. Many conditions may not be found until the child gets older such as Autism.  When people choose to allow their lives to be filled with the laughs and cries of a child, they must also accept the responsibility of care that goes along with it.  Sometimes that responsibility can last a lifetime with a special child.

**Loss of life**.  Today it is rare for a woman to die during pregnancy or delivery, yet it still happens.  Whether it's an aneurism, heart attack or some other unexplainable tragedy it is difficult to understand how something so incredible could result in something so devastating.  There are many risks to the baby during pregnancy and it is a miracle for a child to actually make it to term.  It is very common for a woman to miscarry in the first few weeks of pregnancy and typically the woman never realizes that she was actually pregnant.  But when a woman carries a baby to term and then loses the baby due to some fluke, unforeseen condition or just bad luck, it is not the infant that suffers.  Counseling for both parents should start early, and as she will likely be a wreck, it is up to you to set it up and convince her to go.  It may take years to recover from such a loss and many marriages don't withstand the hardship.

**An unexpected joy**.  Sometimes the things we don't expect aren't so bad.  It is not unheard of that ultrasounds, including the new 3-D sonograms could be wrong about determining the sex of the baby.  While looking into the body through walls of skin, muscle, sinew and fluids at something else has advanced light years, it is still not photographic evidence and what was to be a girl may turn out to be a boy…and vice versa.  Sometimes, that single heartbeat and large baby hid a smaller one behind it, and you are rushing around trying to determine what your second choice names are.

**Post Partum Depression**.  This is a very serious concern as women tend to hide emotions or thoughts that are anything other than happy and excited about having a baby.  The fact is that many women face a depression following the delivery of the baby and for months afterward.  The signs can be as obvious as sleeping too much, however sleeping too little can also be a sign.  Another obvious sign is disinterest in the baby, however overprotection of the baby is also a sign.  You must pay close attention to the mommy when she is with and without the baby and just talk openly and honestly about your feelings and hers.  Sometimes the mommy is just weary from caring for the baby and is not actually depressed.  You need to recognize that for what it is and offer caring and tending to the baby for periods of time.  If you do determine, or if she is afraid that depression is affecting her everyday life, seek counseling support.  Most hospitals have programs specifically designed to work with Post Partum Depression.

**Post Traumatic Stress Syndrome**.  You have been under constant stress from getting the baby's room ready, to running out for ice cream, pickle and sardine parfaits, to rubbing her sore muscles… and now that baby is here you feel like you can just sit back and relax.  However, when the baby cries, you jump and have momentary flashbacks.  Don't worry you are just learning how to be a dad.  Prepare yourself for sleepless nights, arguments over "fair" sharing and caring for the baby and late night runs to the store for diapers or formula.  Therefore, as there is no "after stress" period, you cannot possibly experience "post" stress.  Lucky us, right?  Again, if she hasn't read this, you could reference how fathers sometimes go through this condition and the only cure is a day out on the golf course.

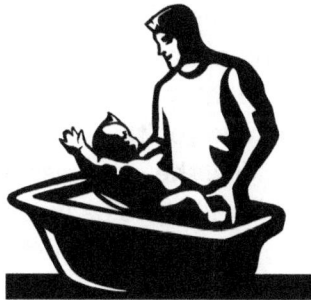

## Chapter 4 - Your New Born...sans new car smell

The first thing to understand about new born babies is that they are just cute.  To other people, they may be wrinkly and grayish and possibly repulsive.  But to new parents the baby is the most beautiful thing ever.  Some say that our brains release chemicals to see the baby as a cute and lovable thing that you want to hold and give kisses to.  Strange but true, just wait.  It has also been theorized that our ancient cave man ancestors needed to feel close to its offspring and were strangely hypnotized by their appearance so babies wouldn't be left out for the wolves...thus the continuation of our species.

Babies had to be especially cute on those late nights in the cave when Tong and Gua spent the day felling a giant wooly mammoth who's tail meat gave you gas and has kept you from sleeping, as little Tong junior starts with his late night bawling... otherwise Tong would have no namesake.

As you admire your little ones toes and fingers, you hear a little grunt.  Your baby is still getting used to air and light and sleeps a lot.  When they are awake, they don't like the experience and the only solace comes from mommas breasts.  (Can't fault them there)  Still, you realize that at some point the baby will poo... all things do... and whose job do you think it is to take care of that little mess?  Hers?  Not likely, she just finished many many hours of labor and is tired and not likely to be up and moving around and definitely not up to the task of diaper changing.  So, armed with your infantile knowledge of diaper changing you take it upon yourself.

You carefully make a flat surface that is soft and covered with a blanket. You lay the baby in the middle, who by now has taken his healthy lungs to cry out loudly because he is getting cold and doesn't like being unswadled. You prepare a new diaper and hands full of wipes and are steadying yourself for having to wipe a butt that is not your own. Holding your breath as the baby wiggles and shakes you unfasten the diaper and open it up.

First thought,...not so bad, just a little black poopie. You take your wipe and try to extricate the poop from the bottom, but it's not coming off. A scene from the Blob comes to your mind as this clingy poop is resistant to your efforts to wipe it off. It is more like tar than poop you notice and then you start to ask yourself, 'if all diapers are going to be this tough, perhaps I should bow out of the diaper changing business altogether'.  You may also begin to worry about the unhuman nature of this black goo that has now stuck to everything and might in fact call for turpentine to extract it from the skin. You decide that the only smart thing to do is press the nurse call button and point out this completely unnatural event. She smiles, pats you on the arm and finishes cleaning the mess telling you that it's normal. In fact it is! It is known as meconium and is your babys' first poo. It's like a concentrated tar that was designed to keep the bottom plugged until after the baby was born. Once that plug is out, the poo never seems to stop. That is a different matter altogether!

Don't worry, the next chapter of this book will discuss how to actually change and clean the baby. We will also cover how to swaddle and how to dress the baby. That being said, your baby is now ready to be placed back into its hospital basinet.

At this point people will come and go and give you all kinds of paperwork to read (like that will happen), and some will come to check on the mommy and baby to make sure things are going fine. Your baby will likely be taken to the nursery for a short time period to be given extra tests, I suspect it has something to do with determining if your child was born a genius or has a propensity for politics. Whatever the tests they give the baby, ultimately they return the child to you. Trust me, no one wants to take your baby home but you. Still, take no chances. Many hospitals utilize an electronic band unit on the mommy and baby to ensure the baby is with the right mommy and isn't being taken out of the maternity ward.

Family and friends will start stopping by to give their greetings, make faces and give kisses to the baby. The mommy will tell the same birthing story to every person who walks in and as she tells it you are surprised at how she can make it sound like it was the first time she told the story. If visitors were to ask the father the story is usually something like this: "It was long, she was in lots of pain, she cussed me out a few times, then the baby came out". There, in ten seconds the delivery story was efficiently and effectively given. The unfortunate fact is that people won't want your version, they will want an hours' worth of gore and detail with climatic points and pauses for effect.

Eventually the visitors stop coming and it is your turn to really get a chance to touch and hold the baby. Mommy has already fed and cuddled with the little one and has started the bonding experience, but we fathers get very little bonding time. So you cradle your little one who is now effectively swaddled and sound asleep. You look at the face and wonder what he or she will look like growing up, you imagine the world you are introducing them to and the opportunities you want to create for them. Sure, they will resent you through their teenage years and will never thank you for all the sacrifices and hard work it took to get them raised...not until they have their own children. That is where becoming a grandparent gives you great pleasure in saying, "see, I told you that it would come back to bite you in the butt".

After a couple of days it is time to go home...unmonitored, no safety net, no nurses, no doctors...you are completely on your own. You start to panic as you have no idea what to do now that it's time to go home. Don't panic, the following section provides a quick reference detailing how to care for babies now that you are all alone.

Just remember, the baby doesn't know that you are clueless and don't know what you're doing. Just stay confident and refer to the next section often. Babies can smell your fear and pick up on your tentative actions...give a baby some rope and they will tie a lasso, rope your legs and pull you down. Sure, the baby mama won't believe you but it's all true ☺

**You can also check out further series of the Daddy Survival Guide including the one covering the baby's first year and afterward dealing with the toddler years.**

Part III – Life's little instruction book for a dad with no clue on what to do with a baby.., someone at the hospital should have stopped you at the door and made you take a practical exam before allowing you to go home...

**Instruction 1 – Installing and testing a Car Seat**

1.  Make sure the car seat is located in the back seat and if possible in the center
2. The car seat should be rear facing (the baby should be facing the rear window of the car)
3. If the car seat has a level meter on the side, make sure you adjust the seat so that the level is in the green or safe area
4. Some car seats have a removable base, make sure to use the seat belt as described in the product handbook to secure it in place
5. There should be an extra reinforcement strap that gets attached to metal hooks in your car, you may need to refer

to your car manual as these are not always easy to find, once you do find them you start to wonder why you never noticed those before
6. Make sure you shake, pull and attempt to move the car seat or base to ensure it is stable (NOTE: Do not do this with baby in the seat)
7. If you are using a removable base, the car seat should snap securely on top of the base, familiarize yourself with how to snap the car seat in place and how to remove it (This should be easy)
8. If you have two cars, it is a good idea to have a removable base for each car
9. Familiarize yourself with the strapping mechanisms, look for obvious hazards that the baby may able to reach or may restrict the baby in a way that was not designed by the product

**Instruction 2 – Putting baby in a car seat**

1. Practice with a life sized doll before attempting to strap a live baby into a car seat. It is simple once you've done it a few hundred times
2. Babies are often swaddled which make it difficult to use a 5 point seat belt system, however you can just strap them in as though they had no feet, the restraining system is designed to work anyway
3. If you do have the baby with free legs, one should go on each side of the center buckle
4. The shoulder straps should start just below the baby's shoulders and go up and over them to be connect to the center buckle

5.  The side straps should come around the front of the baby, above the legs and below the arms to again connect to the center buckle
6.  Once all the buckles have been fastened, tighten the straps just enough to keep the baby from moving out of the restraints.  (Tightening the straps may be challenging, look for a car seat that has an easy  tighten and loosen mechanism.  It will make this task that much easier).  While the baby is a newborn they will not likely slip out of their restraints, it's when they are two years old that I have a whole new book on how to keep children in places where they refuse to be...like in car seats when you are driving 65 MPH on the interstate.
7.  Always pull on the restraints and buckles to make sure your connection is solid.
8.  If you are using a base with removable seat, it's just good practice to strap the baby in even if you are not putting the baby in the car.  The straps will keep the baby from squirreling out of their baby prison

Car seats are important safety devices and should be taken seriously.  It is highly recommended that once you install your car seat, and prior to putting your baby in to it, take it down to a state police or fire station to have someone look at it and give you the thumbs up.   I have no recommendations on brands or makes of car seats, I have used many over the years.  I will tell you that it doesn't hurt to do some internet searches to find ones that had recent recall issues, and then steer clear of those ☺.  And while used may be cheaper, sometimes it's just better to buy a newer product that has been tested thoroughly.

NOTE:  There are few things I read the product information on, however I would always recommend that this be in your short reading list – the instruction manual for the car seat you purchase.

## Instruction 3 – Using a Stroller

1. Like car seats there are many models and styles and finding the right one is not an easy task. You want to make sure it rolls easily, is very maneuverable and height adjustable. My wife is just over 5 feet tall and I am just over 6 foot. Our comfortable arm height is different (by a foot) so for us to use the same stroller, one or the other is not going to be happy. Fortunately many strollers are made with adjustable handles.

2. Most strollers fold up. It is important that you practice <u>without the baby</u> on the proper way to fold and unfold your stroller. Most have a turning handled at the top

where you push that when turned will start the stroller folding. Others have releases on the metal poles on either side of where the baby sits, these releases are typically triggered by pulling a lever. And still some have a metal bar at the bottom that allows you to push or pull with your foot to start the folding process. Make sure you fold and unfold several times. There should also be a locking device that allows you to keep the unit from unfolding. Find that and familiarize yourself with how to use it.

3. Some strollers will accept the removable car seat allowing you to just latch it in the stroller the way you do in the base in the car. This makes moving baby from car to stroller very simple.

4. If you are using the stroller itself to transport your baby, make sure you locate the device that allows the back to lower into a laying position. Newborn infants cannot hold their heads and bodies up and need to lay down when transported in this conveyance.

5. Never hang anything from the push handles of the stroller. They are notorious for tipping over as the units tend to balance on the rear wheels. Stores sell wonderful hooks so moms can connect their purses to the handles, but anyone who has used these can tell you that if you use a heavy enough bag, it <u>will</u> tip over.

6. Umbrella strollers are wonderfully lightweight and fold into almost nothing. These are absolutely **not** recommended for infants! (Same rules apply as above, an infant cannot hold themselves in that position.) These are designed for toddlers, but between you, me and everyone who reads this, I don't recommend the cheap version, they simply don't work well. There are Swedish made umbrella type strollers that work wonderfully, and as I cannot name names, I would tell you to do a little shopping and you will find that you pay more for the small form factor, but it is well worth the investment...unless you intend on carrying your toddlers on your shoulders everywhere you go.

7. Strollers, like car seats, have straps. It is always recommended that you tie those little rugrats in, because no matter how wonderful you think your child is, they will find a way to get out and wreak havoc! Of course, straps are good for safety too.

**Instruction 4 – Setting up a playpen**

1. A playpen can be as simple as some couch cushions sitting up on their sides blocking off all exits from the living room, to a complicated multichannel metal contraption that is more likely to take a finger in the assembly/disassembly of the product.
2. Playpens are used primarily to keep baby in a specific place and out of trouble or from getting accidently stepped on. It's also a good place to keep children away from curious pets or other children. It should be set up out of a traffic area to keep people from blindly walking or falling into it.
3. Most playpens have 4 legs that when assembling should be pulled away from the center so there is an open space at the top.
4. The legs are likely connected by a padded bent rod. When straightened out they should lock to form an ... unbent rod, do this all around the opening. You may need to move the legs further apart to keep the playpen square
5. Your playpen should look complete, however there should also be a solid floor that unfolds and goes into the bottom (cushion side up). This is the play area.
6. Make sure there are no holes in the netting (children can get things caught in holes and it isn't pretty).
7. Now, when disassembling you may find that you cannot fold the arms, even through you've worked in reverse order... today's playpens have a safety feature to keep kids from getting caught in the bends and becoming injured.
8. After removing the bottom of the playpen, push the bottom of the feet inward, this will tell the playpen that you are folding.

9. In the center of each rod should be a push button release. Hold it as you push down and the bent arm should form again. Repeat for the other sides and pull the unit together in its folded configuration.
10. As always, read the user manual for actual instructions

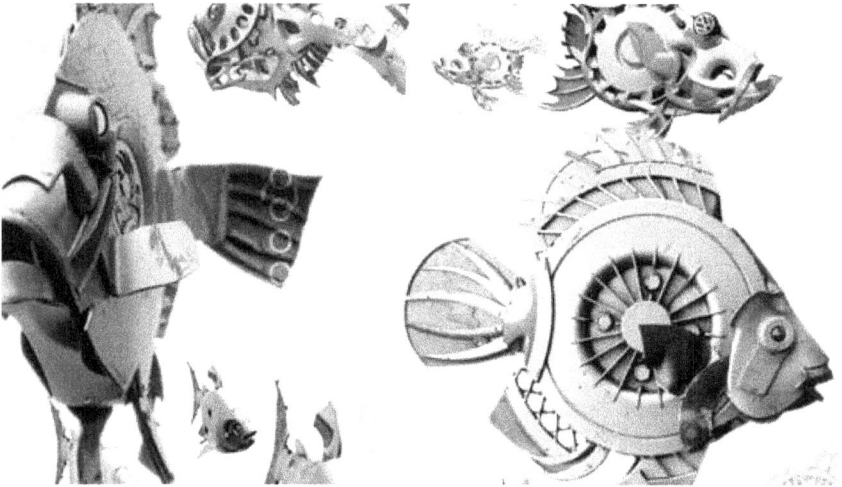

**(It was too difficult to install a fish tank in a book, but at this point you probably need to relax and watch the calming fish)**

**Instruction 5 – Setting up a Cradle or  Bassinette**

1. A bassinette is used primarily for the first few months after the baby is born.  Some call them cradles, but it can be seen as just a small crib.  They are good while the baby is just starting to nurse and needs to be up every two hours (Yes, this is the time in your life that you will look like death for lack of sleep)
2. A bassinette typically is set on a stand to keep the baby off the floor; a cradle typically sits on the floor.  Typically both rock allowing you to soothe the baby back to sleep.
3. Most cradles come fully assembled.  Bassinettes typically have instructions on how to build the stand and cradle portion.  Make sure to have all the tools, screws and parts ready before getting started.  It is helpful to read the instructions as you don't want the thing flipping over with the baby in it.
4. Most bassinettes have a locking mechanism to keep the thing from rocking.  This makes it much easier to get the baby in and out.  Make sure you test your assembly by rocking it, shaking it, locking it in place.  Put something like a bowling ball in it to make sure it's stable.
5. At the base of the bassinette or cradle there should be a pad to make it comfortable for sleeping.
6. Make sure the pad is covered with a fitted sheet.  Never put pillows, stuffed animals or blankets in a cradle or bassinette.  The baby doesn't need them and it can contribute to Sudden Infant Death Syndrome (SIDS).  If it's cool, just dress the baby warmer or zip them up in a very cool invention called a sleeper bag.  It fits over their clothes and it's like a blanket that zips up like a jacket.  Toasty!
7.

## Instruction 6 – Setting up a crib

1. This will likely be one of the most important man jobs you will be given in the whole preparing for baby project. It is important to inventory all the components, instructions and tools to build the crib.
2. First, it is always best to have help! For some reason, the people who design these things don't make it easy for one person to do, so you end up balancing pieces while trying to screw them together
3. Typically the back piece and side pieces are assembled together to make a U formation
4. The spring is then screwed into place before putting in the front rail. There should be adjustment holes to allow you to raise and lower the mattress level. Newborns should be at the highest level to make it easier for the mommy to take the baby out. As they get older you will need to move the mattress down to keep them from crawling over the rail.
5. The front rail often has bars to allow the rail to be raised or lowered making it easier to get the baby out. Great in concept, but I have yet to see one that works well. Ultimately you just pick up the baby and never move the rail.
6. Again, shake rattle and roll the thing after assembly. Make sure it is stable
7. You will probably need to hang a dust ruffle on top of the springs and over the sides to make it "pretty". Again, I have no advice here other than to just not argue and do it.
8. Before putting the mattress on the bed, cover it with a fitted sheet first. You should find sheet holders that are like stretchy fabric with clips on each end. These keep the sheets from coming undone. You will find in the future, it is always easier to change the crib sheet by removing the

mattress rather than trying to dig down on the sides of the crib to tuck it in.

9. The same rules apply for putting the baby in the crib as the cradle and bassinette.  The baby does not need pillows, blankets or stuffed animals.  Just dress them warmly and they should be good to go, if you are still swaddling, that would be acceptable as is the blanket bag.
10. Always remember to lay babies on their backs when putting them to bed!  Lying babies on their back to sleep is believed to prevent SIDS, so just remember **back to sleep**.
11. Make sure there are no strings or loose obstructions that the baby can grab on to.

**Instruction 7 – Crib Accoutrements**

1. Mobiles are fun little devices that screw on to the rear rail of the crib.  They typically wind up and play music.  These are great until babies can pull themselves up and yank them down.  There are many recommendations on the best ones to buy, but it really is up to personal taste.  Babies just like sound and motion.  They are typically not concerned over whether it plays Mozart or Humpty Dumpty.
2. Side mounted play toys are great when it's time to remove the mobile.  These allow the child to activate lights and music by pressing, pulling and pushing little buttons.  This too hooks on to the rails of the crib and like all child toys, takes batteries that die way too soon!

3. Crib Tents are often unseen at your local baby store, but a real concern is that your

wonderful pets may be a little too curious about the baby. An old wives tale would state that a cat steals the breath from a baby, and the baby dies. The truth is that cats enjoy lying on thing, people, babies... and love to sniff at the milk breath baby has without realizing that its weight is enough to suffocate the baby. A crib tent installs inside the rails of the crib and has a zipper or opening to remove the baby, while keeping curious felines out. This is one of those devices that is a good precautionary tool and falls under the adage, "better safe than sorry." Admittedly, they are a pain to when you have a sleeping baby and you go to zip it closed and the loud zipping noise wakes the baby right up. On the other hand it keeps the baby in the crib in the event that you have a crib escape artist.

## Instruction 8 – Setting up a Swing

1. A hundred years ago a poor mother, sibling or if you were well to do, nanny would pace the floor rocking the baby to soothe the never ceasing tears. At some point a genius man built a swing to mimic the motion of rocking
2. By the middle of the 20th century, swings with wind up mechanisms were touted as the best purchase any new parent could make, and the statement still holds true today. Some people think that it won't be a problem to pick the baby up and rock it when it's fussy...those are naïve people or saints. It does not hurt the baby to put them in a swing, as long as the baby is calmed by the motion. However, there is the rare baby who doesn't like the motion.
3. Most swings move forward and back and have adjustable seats that can be laid back or sat forward. There are some higher end ones that move side to side for infants and forward and back for older children. These are probably

better, but the price tag makes them cost prohibitive, so the standard forward and back motion is adequate.

4. Swings come 90% assembled and the final assembly is a matter of snapping legs into place. The baby's mother doesn't need to know how easy it is and you may want to take your time setting the unit up.

5. Swings can be either manual wind up or battery operated. I highly recommend the latter. After an exhausting night with my daughter, the swing pacified her to sleep, however as soon as the spring ran out of energy the swing would stop and she would start to cry meaning that I would have to get up and wind it up every 3 minutes. Battery units are better, and most new swings have a timer to run for a period of time then stop.

6. A swing is not a baby sitter and should not be used as the place to put baby because you are "busy". They are just temporary relief or to help an especially fussy baby to stop crying

7. By the time the baby is big enough to grab the bars on the side of the swing to stop herself, it is time to get rid of it.

8. Swings can tip over. Despite the manufacturers insistence that it is not probable, if the swing moves too fast and too high and the baby is overly active, the swing can definitely fall over. Swings need to be monitored for speed, baby comfort and proper motion. If any of these don't seem right, don't put the baby in it.

9. Last and especially important, an infant should only be put in a swing if the seat is in a laid back position and set to a slow speed. Watch to make sure the baby's head isn't rocking forward and back or in an awkward position.

10. Finally, always belt the baby in the seat for safety.

## Instruction 9 – Setting up a bouncy seat

1. I have to admit that I went through 5 children before my last actually had one of these handy little devices. The design is similar to a swing, except they just bounce, are small and low to the ground and don't typically swing
2. When running over to friends or family, a swing is a big item to tote around, but you want to have something other than the car seat to put the baby in, and many times you don't want to just let baby crawl all over some strange floor...eww
3. Bouncy seats are typically fully assembled, but usually can be folded down by rotating the bottom legs or removing them. (Refer to your instruction guide)
4. Make sure you belt in baby!
5. Some seats have vibration and sound. Just gauge if your baby actually likes that or not.
6. Babies enjoy the movement of a bouncy seat and are often entertained by them when they are awake.
7. Bouncy seats are also great to feed babies in while they are still too young for high chairs

## Instruction 10 – Setting up a monitor

1. Finally, a chance to act like a spy. Baby monitors are one way devices that allow you to listen in on the activity in the baby room via radio waves.
2. One unit should be plugged in the room where the baby sleeps. It does not need to be right next to the baby as they are very sensitive and pick up noise easily. The other

is typically battery powered and can be carried with you anywhere.

3. Check the range on your monitor. The easiest way to do this is to play a music CD in the baby's room and close the door. Then walk around the house, garage, yard and beyond to see what the range is, if you have dead areas where you cannot hear anything on the monitor, make sure to clearly mark those areas or try a different monitor

4. Some monitors have an option to only produce while others can show a led display to identify noise activity and others actually vibrate. Vibrating monitors are good when you are doing something that might overpower the sound or if you cannot see the lights.

5. Video monitors are becoming more popular now and some even come with night vision to allow you to see the baby without needing to have the lights on. These video monitors have receivers that can be worn on your wrist like a watch, carried like a walkie talkie or connected to your television. Some are black and white and others are color. Again it's up to how much money you want to spend on coolness.

6. The downside of video monitors is that they operate on radio waves and depending on how close your neighbors are (and if they a device like yours) you could actually be watching their baby and they yours.

7. Remember, video cameras leave an open door to voyeurs and you are sacrificing privacy.

8. Of course once the baby is done using it, I am sure there are other spy tasks you can perform by strategically relocating the transmitter unit.

## Instruction 11 – Setting up a baby bath & bathing

1. Babies do not need to be washed every day. You should make some judgment on when to clean the baby. Typically spot cleaning is more effective like under the chin where milk may trickle to and get all funky. It's a good idea to clean there. You will notice areas that need cleaning, so pay special attention to your technique.

2. Pick a bathing location: Most people prefer the kitchen sink. First because it's higher and easier to work at than in the bath tub or on the bath sink. Avoid using the sprayer or spicket on the baby, the water temperature is difficult to control and it is not a good idea to make the baby hot or cold. Just have the water ready ahead of time. Fill the tub with ½" of water and have an 8 oz cup or two with water of the same temperature as the tub. The temperature should be warmer than room temperature and not as warm as body temperature. Check with your elbow to see if it feels "warm", not hot or cold.

3. When your newborn first comes home, you are probably thinking you want to dunk them into a clean bath to get all those hospital germs off…don't. Until the umbilical cord falls off, you should not put your baby in any bath.

4. Newborns can easily be washed by using a rag and small basin with warm water. You want to wet the rag and lightly wash each area of the baby's body taking care to wipe downward and away. Only uncover the area that you are going to clean so you don't make the baby cold. Pay special attention to the area around the umbilical cord, and it is recommended that you use an alcohol wipe to clean around the belly button until the cord falls off. When washing around the eyes, just take the edge of the wet rag and wipe from the tear duct out on both the top

and bottom lid. When actually the baby, you should work in order from around the eyes first, then the mouth, head, ears, neck, torso arms, legs hands and finally feet.

5. For babies without the umbilical cord, there are a number of baby baths that can be used to lay the baby in with some warm water. Use only baby wash to soap up the water and fill the bottom with just a small amount of water. Use a rag to clean the baby, and a cup of warm water to rinse the baby off.

6. Babies will love or hate the water. Just don't get frustrated, keep your head down and do the cleaning quickly and efficiently.

7. Babies will pee and poop in the bath. They don't control their waste functions so they do it whenever they feel the need. The best plan is to wash quickly

8. Babies don't need toys in the bath, when they are old enough they will drag their own toys into the bath, until then they are not necessary. However, when they are old enough, you may want to monitor what toys they take in the bath with them...big no's include toys with batteries, stuffed animals, books and daddy's collection of 1970s Star Trek figurines

9. **Never leave a baby alone for any period of time in a bath,** babies have a knack for doing the one thing you don't want them too. It only takes ½" of water at the bottom of a bath for a baby to drown. It is better to have everything you need next to you before starting the bath.

10. When removing baby from the bath, make sure you immediately wrap them in a towel to keep them warm

11. Babies don't need oils or baby powder unless a doctor recommends it. Babies produce enough of their own skin byproducts to keep themselves soft and smooth. The baby mama may think it's nice to use baby powder because it makes the baby smell good, unfortunately the baby's smeller can get plugged up with the powder and breathed into the lungs which is not so nice.

12. After using light strokes to dry the baby, diaper quickly...again, they will pee or poop if given the opportunity. Do not carry them around the house hoping you will make it to the changing table. And if you decide to diaper the baby on the counter or dining table, never leave the baby alone... even if they are not supposed to roll on their sides for months, they still manage to wiggle around and can fall!! (Diapering instructions are included in the next step)
13. Dress your baby so that they are comfortable. (Dressing is also in another step.)
14. Notify the baby's mother that you washed the baby and put the baby down somewhere safe. By telling her that you did the task, she will know not to do it again and you should get points for doing a chore. It's important that you consciously identify that you indeed "help" with the baby as mommies often forget that certain chores are done by you...taking out the trash, cleaning up dog poo, cleaning out the garage... You may also want to track diaper changes, clothing, feeding... Again it is important for men to identify that they have "helped" and you may need to produce the tracking document to prove it. Of course she will give you grief regardless and express that she does far more, but that is really not the point. Right?!

**Instruction 12 – Diapers and the Agony of Defeat**

1. First, understand that it is a dirty job and no one wants to do it. If you find that someone volunteers because they find it wonderful, quickly kick that person out of your house because they are obviously unstable. If it happens to be your mother in law, you may also need to take out a restraining order.
2. You need certain tools to complete the task of diapering. The first is a changing table, table, couch, bed or floor. It

really doesn't matter where you change the baby.  She may tell you different, but if it matters that much to her, she can change the baby herself.  I have always preferred the floor.  Regardless of where you choose to change the baby, check for safety first.  Make sure the space is unobstructed with things the baby can grab or that can be knocked over.  Make sure the space is level so the baby doesn't roll away; couches are notorious for sucking in change and babies.

3.  Lay something down on the changing area, even if you use a changing table, it's easier to wash a towel or burp cloth if it gets soiled.  Make sure the item is soft and absorbent, that way if the baby pees midstream of changing it will suck up the urine.

4.  It is documented that men change babies at an average of 2 minutes 35 seconds and women change them in 3 minutes 15 seconds.  First because men are better at it, second because men just get the work done and last, women like to talk... a lot... and if the baby is the only one around she will talk to the baby and multitasking while talking is not typically a strong suit of women. (Remember, this is a confidential men only book.  Do not share this well known and documented fact with a woman.  You are just asking for a fight.)

5.  Make sure you have wipes pulled out of the container (at least 2) and ready to use.  The container should be ready for you to pull out more in the event that it is a full release and the baby stuff goes everywhere.  Wipes should be moist and free of dyes and perfumes, it is just safer on the baby as their skin is especially sensitive.

6.  You must make a choice of disposable or cloth diapers.  I won't argue one way or the other, but see the survival tip to make your own decision on the matter.  If you are using disposable, have one open with the tabs away from you sticky side up as these will go to the back of the baby.  If you are using cloth with Velcro, position the spiny side up

the same as the disposable diaper. If you are using cloth with safety pins, put this book down and go to the store and buy products from this millennia. By having the diaper open, as soon as you pull the soiled diaper away, you can place the new one underneath thereby limiting the possibility of baby refuse unloading at an inopportune moment.

7. Place the baby in front of you and strip the clothing from the belly button down, make sure this clothing is out of the way as inevitably poo and pee will find their way to them. You may need to pull up shirts and onsies to get them clear of the danger zone.

8. Be quick, be thorough, be efficient.

9. Unstrap the Velcro or tape from the front of the diaper and lay them out to the side of the baby.

10. Quickly open and close the front of the diaper to see what you are dealing with, based on what you see you can decide if you need more wipes at the ready (practice will tell you the right number to have on hand.)

11. You should practice changing diapers on a doll!

12. Open the messy diaper and fold the front down to the table.

13. With your non-wiping hand, you need to hold both feet at the ankles keeping them a couple of inches apart and not holding too tightly. Then lift them and the baby's bottom in the air.

14. Wipe the poo area first making sure you work in a front to back motion, throw the dirty wipe into the open dirty diaper, repeat as necessary.

15. Once all the poo is cleaned away, with the wiping hand close the diaper and move it to the side. Place the clean opened diaper in its place and lay the babys bottom on top of it, be careful because this is the point where they baby can pee on you!

16. Next wipe the front area of the baby, if you have a girl make sure you wipe only front to back and clean all the folds.  Again put the wipes on top of the dirty diaper.

17. If you have a boy, be prepared with the clean diaper in an open position.  Boys are notorious for squirting!!  If you are weirded out by the possibility of squirting, there are protective cup devices that you can use to keep the stream from wandering everywhere.

18. Once baby is clean, fold the front portion of the diaper back over the front.  It should make a U shape from the back to the front of the baby.  Use the sticky tape or Velcro from the back and pull them to secure the diaper in the front.  The diaper should be snug, like when you tighten your belt to hold up your pants.

19. Before continuing you should use some hand sanitizer to kill any germs you may have gotten on your hands during the "Diaper Incident"

20. Dress the baby paying particular attention to not touch the old diaper.

21. Take the old diaper and dump the wipes into a bag, then rinse the diaper out in the toilet before throwing it out or putting into a laundry basket (gross I know, but I have to support a cleaner, greener planet)

**Survival Baby Tip: Cloth versus Disposable Diapers**

Arguments on both side of this discussion exists:

1. Environmental nuts will tell you that cloth is preferred as it keeps disposable diapers out of landfills where their half life is 200 years. That means it will take 400 years to be dust.
2. Lazy moms and dads will tell you that it's a pain to wash out cloth diapers, they leak, they stink and we waste water to clean them which causes a bigger impact to the environment.
3.

**Skin & Health Issues** – 54% of babies using disposable diapers get rashes, dyes and perfumes can cause toxic shock and headaches, other chemicals from the gel to bleaching material can create caustic smells, tape if improperly affixed can tear skin. The key to reducing diaper rash is to keep wetness and bacteria away from the skin which disposable diapers can do. Cloth diapers, even with plastic lining, triple thickness and inserts can still cause rashes unless they are changed as soon as the baby urinates and cleaned properly after every use to reduce bacteria.

**Cost** – Disposable Diapers will cost $50 - $80 a month, a diaper service will cost $50 - $80 a month, if you launder cloth diapers instead of using a service the cost comes down to $25 - $60 a month.

**Environment** - Roughly 5 million tons of untreated waste and a total of 2 billion tons of urine, feces, plastic and paper are added to landfills annually. It takes around 80,000 pounds of plastic and over 200,000 trees a year to manufacture the disposable diapers for American babies alone.  Some disposable diapers are identified as biodegradable, but they require oxygen and sunlight to do so which is highly unlikely in a landfill.  Landfill elements have also been identified as polluting ground fill water.  Water used to rinse and clean cloth diapers contribute to water usage by two to three times of flushing a toilet per diaper (it takes a couple of flushes to get the big stuff out, then washing them adds 1 to 2 laundry loads a week.  Water that gets pushed into sewers are treated and redistributed as clean water.

On a positive note, companies have been using disposable diapers as an alternate fuel source that burns cleaner than coal.  Of course there are no regular pick up points.  Also, new cloth diapers have disposable inserts that can be flushed down toilets eliminating the need to rinse the poop out.  In the end, the baby and you will need to figure out what works best.  Some people who use cloth diapers still like the convenience of a disposable diaper when out and about or traveling as it's much easier to throw out than carry around a soiled diaper.

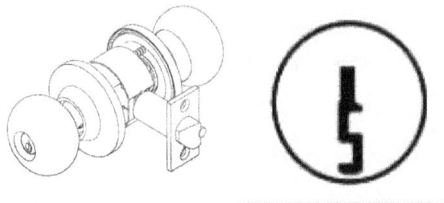

**Survival Daddy Tip:  Picking a Lock**
I will never admit to locking myself out of the house while the baby was inside, but if I had, I would have had these choices:  Break a window, call my mother to drive a key to the house or pick the lock.

Lock picking is not as simple as they make it seem on television and it does take some practice.  But as you read this far along and you want to understand how locking mechanisms work, I might as well tell you how to get past a standard cylinder lock.  First, you will two tools, a rake and a turning rod.  The rake is a piece of metal that looks like a dentist pick, the other is just a nail file.  Both need to be thin enough to fit into the keyway.  The turning tool needs to be inserted at the opposite end of where the teeth of the key go.  The Rake will be used to run across the cylinder pins, the same way the teeth on a key does.  With the turning rod in place turn until the cylinder gives some resistance then starting at the back run the rake across the pins pulling it toward you.  By keeping the cylinder turning with resistance, at least one of the pins should have locked out of the way, Continue the process until all the pins have been opened and you can turn the cylinder.  Tools, and practice are the key to doing it right.

Do not attempt to try this on a car, newer technology makes it practically unpickable.  The standard is still a hanger through the door jamb and hope to hit the unlock button or break a window.  If you happen to lock your baby in the car, you may not have time to think about it, especially if it's hot out.  Look around for a rock or something hard and bread out one of the door windows furthest away from the baby.  It will cost about $200 to replace and an afternoon, but is worth the cost to have your baby safe and sound!

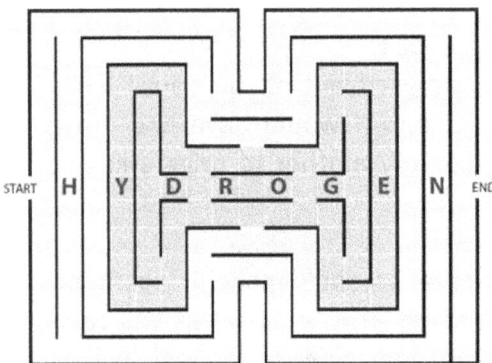

**To solve this puzzle, draw a line through the maze touching every letter, you cannot pass through the same section or cross over a line.**

**Instruction 13 – Dressing up baby**

1. Regardless how much encouragement she gives you to pick out an outfit and clothe your baby, you will get it wrong 9 out of 10 times.  Play it safe with light neutral colors and unless you are going out, dress the baby in a sleeper.
2. Understand the Lingo:
    a. Onesie – A unitard for babies.  This one piece usually short sleeve T-Shirt that extends down over the diaper and snaps at the bottom.  This helps keep diapers on and covers the belly!  A onesie should always be your base to start dressing from other than the diaper.
    b. Sleeper – Typically this is a one piece snap on or zip up outfit with footies to cover the baby's feet.  If you are dressing the baby in something without footies, you will need to put socks on the baby.
    c. Layette – These look like sleepers at the top and a bag at the bottom.  This allows the baby free range of movement, and saves you from trying to stick tiny legs into the legs of a sleeper
    d. Outfit – A clothing combination that should match...this is a danger zone for most men
3. Babies will also need socks, possibly mittens and stocking caps.
4. You should always dress baby just a little warmer than yourself.  If you go outside without a T-Shirt and feel comfortable, baby should be in a onesie.  If you are comfortable in a shirt, the baby can be in a light sleeper or outfit.  Socks are almost always a good idea unless it's stinking hot outside.  If it is cool out (less than 75 degrees Fahrenheit), put a cap on the baby's head, they tend to lose heat much faster than we do.  Be careful not to overdress, if you feel comfortable in your clothes, they

baby should be dressed similarly to feel comfortable in theirs.

5. Be careful of zippers. Babies move a lot and their little bodies and skin are extremely sensitive. When zipping up a zipper, pull up and away from the baby so you don't accidently grab the skin. The fabric when you are zipping should not be touching skin.

6. Make sure clothing is not too big or small for the baby. If the baby needs to scrunch up to put on a onesie, it is too small. If you can fit most of your baby's body into the sleeve of the sports team jacket you purchased, it's probably too big.

7. Clothing should always be cleaned even if it is new. Use the no dyes or perfume types of laundry detergent to avoid any rashes or allergy issues.

8. When putting a sleeper (The thing with footies) hold the baby up against you and put the feet of the sleeper on the baby first. Then as you are laying the baby down, carefully with one hand spread out the sleeper under the baby and lay the baby on top of it. (I shouldn't have to tell you that the sleeper needs to be unbuttoned or unzipped first) The zipper typically is opened all the way down to one ankle, zip it up to the diaper before putting the arms in. Then, one arm at a time, cover the baby's hand with your own and work it most of the way through the sleeve. With your other hand reach into the opening of the sleeve and lightly grab the baby's hand and pull it through. Do the same from the other side. Remember to pull the zipper up and away from the baby.

9. Other outfits may require a combination of holding the baby, laying down, turning over and all kinds of baby acrobats to get them on. Always be cautious of little baby hands and feet and make sure you lead them into the openings so little fingers and toes don't get stuck and broken.

**Instruction 14 – Swaddling**

1. Newborns are accustomed to living in very tight quarters, and after 9 months of limited space they are a little freaked out by free movement. It's not quite agoraphobia, but to a new born it is very upsetting.
2. Swaddling is a fancy term for wrapping a baby's body tight with a towel or blanket, paying special attention to fastening the arms and legs close to the body.
3. Lay a receiving blanket on a bed. The blanket will likely be rectangular, and while a square blanket would work better, you can still swaddle effectively with a rectangular blanket. The blanket should be the size of a smaller bath towel. Fold down the top corner, this is the point where the neck will go
4. Practice with a doll first before trying this on your newborn.
5. Carefully lay the baby centered diagonally on the blanket resting the neck on the fold. You do not want to saddle above the neck.
6. Take the short side on the left and fold it over the baby, it should feel snug but not tight. You may need to tuck it in under the baby. If you have too much material, use a smaller blanket or fold the blanket in half first.
7. Take the bottom corner and pull it up to the neck, you want to get the feet pulled up slightly. If you have too much material, fold the excess at the neckline and take the material and run it along the side of the body.
8. Take the right corner, and pull all the extra fabric and wrap it around the baby. It should be snug, not tight. You can find a crevice to tuck in the end of the flap.

9. Most times an effective swaddling will help comfort a fussy baby. Once a child starts moving around enough to scoot or turn, they will no longer need to be swaddled.

## Instruction 15 – Feeding

1. Newborns need only formula or breast milk. This is all they will eat for six months. They will start by taking only small portions and will work up to larger. A newly born baby will only eat as much as the size of a marble. Within a week they will be eating up to the size of a walnut.
2. Feeding time is often argued by parents as to when, how much, whether or not you should wake the baby or wait for them to want to eat. At first, you will need to encourage the baby to eat. While they may be hungry, they haven't learned how to ask for food yet. Within a month or two, they will start letting you know through motions or noises that they are hungry.
3. With newborns it is best to feed every 2 to 2 ½ hours. Remember that they are only consuming tiny portions. As they eat more, they need to be fed less often.
4. Bottle fed babies tend to eat a lot more food sooner, however they also tend to have much more throw up than a breast fed baby. Think of chugging down a pitcher of beer, sure you could probably do it, but it is also likely some of that is going to come back up. Bottle fed babies typically chug their bottles. To keep them from taking too much at one time, there are different nipples that go on the bottle. Newborn nipples should have few or tiny holes to allow a slow express of the liquid. There are other nipples with more and larger holes for the baby as they get larger and can take in more fluids. The woman's breast will supply as much milk as the baby requires. If the baby

needs more, more is created. It's a strange chemical mystery (Oxytocin Hormone)

5. This book will not give you instructions on how to breast feed. We are men and simply do not have the tools to do that kind of work. However, if she does breastfeed, she can express her milk into bottles allowing you the opportunity to feed the baby too.

6. As a dad if you are bottle feeding you need some tools:
    a. A burp cloth – Just a fancy towel to throw over your shoulder so that when you burp the baby it won't puke all over your clothes
    b. A bottle with breast milk or formula and an appropriate nipple. Remember, the nipple should have only tiny holes and should not allow much to come through
    c. A baby. Preferably one that is awake and ready to eat

7. When a newborn comes home and you are ready to feed them, remember the size of their stomach. Bottles are graduated to show you how much fluid is contained inside. At first 2 to 4 ounces will be fed. You will need to keep track of how much you are feeding the baby so the mom and doctor have a sense if it is too much or too little.

8. While there are pros and cons to all bottle models and styles, my personal favorite is the kind that comes with a disposable bag to put the milk in to (and by milk I mean baby formula or breast milk, NOT cows milk). After filling the bottle with liquid, you can press up underneath the bag to let all the air out. No air = less gas and less barfing. Also, when the baby finishes eating, you can throw the insert out and only have the nipple to clean. Men aren't lazy, just practical.

9. Mixing formula can be one of the biggest challenges for dads. You should be aware that there are premixed formula products that can be stored at room temperature and just poured in to a bottle and you are ready to go!

There are also concentrated liquids that need to be mixed with water before pouring in to the bottle. This takes a little more skill as you have to read the correct proportions, but gives you a great reason to pull out the martini shaker. Powder is about the same as concentrate except it takes a little more effort to mix. By far the best value comes from powder, but it requires the most work. With concentrate or powder, it's a good idea to make a days worth of formula and pour it into bottles ahead of time so you just have to go in to the refrigerator and pull one out to serve the baby.

10. **Warming bottles**. If you are serving formula already at room temperature, there is no need to warm them. If you pull one from the refrigerator, DO NOT microwave it. The bottle won't explode, but the formula may heat uneven and you may think it's room temperature but there could be a cloud of scalding hot formula in the bottle that could hurt the baby. If it's breast milk you're warming up it could also change the chemical makeup of the milk. The best method is to fill a pan with warm (100 degrees Fahrenheit) water and put the bottle in it for 5 to 10 minutes. Feel the bottle and drop a little on the back of your hand. It should not feel cold.

11. Make sure you have a comfortable spot to sit in that you can easily stand up without using your hands. There are times when you have the baby over your shoulder and you need to stand quickly... like when you forget which side to put the burp cloth on and the baby pukes warm milk all down your back.

12. **Now Lets Feed**
    a. Burp cloth goes over the shoulder you plan to burp baby on
    b. Bottle within reach
    c. Pick up the baby by putting your hand behind their head and your other hand under their butt

d. Put the baby's head and shoulders in the crook of your elbow
e. Make sure to keep baby covered and warm
f. The baby should be at a 40 degree angle with the feet lower than the head
g. Take the bottle and put the nipple to the baby's mouth. They should open their mouth and allow you to put the nipple in gently. The baby should take it in and start sucking immediately.
h. If the baby doesn't open their mouth, try running the nipple across their lips to help them understand that it's time to eat
i. If they still don't open, take your finger and gently push it into their mouth to get them to open up and realize there is food
j. While your baby is eating they are also breathing. You and I cannot do this little trick. While they are still babies the windpipe and esophagus are separated allowing babies to feed without coming up for air. Just be mindful that their nose is clear and not loaded with boogies! If there are boogies, you should have a little bulb syringe that you probably got at the hospital. Push in the ball then put the open end into the baby's nose. Let go of the pushed in part and it will suction out the boogie. It may take some practice.
k. If a baby cries as you start to feed, there may be another problem.
   i. Check to see if the milk is coming out of the nipple. Babies get frustrated when they expect food and none comes out
   ii. Check the temperature again. It should be slightly warmer than room temperature
   iii. Try burping the baby to see if they have some unresolved reflux or gas
   iv. Check to see if the baby's diaper needs to be changed

     v.     Try soothing the baby by walking or rocking before attempting to feed again

l. As you feed the baby, you will need to stop every 10 to 15 minutes to burp. Babies eat as quickly as possible and it's like drinking a root beer, it bubbles in the stomach creating burps.

m. Burp the baby

    i.     Put the bottle down first.

    ii.     Take the baby from the crook of your arm, making sure to hold the head and neck and lay the baby on your shoulder and chest

    iii.     It is far safer to turn the baby's head away from your face, sometimes the burps get a little messy

    iv.     The hand of the shoulder the baby is laying on should be holding the baby and balancing them on the shoulder. The best place to position your hand is in the small of the baby's back

    v.     With the other hand opened, pat firmly but not hard on the center of the baby's back just below the shoulder blades. You will need to start soft and work up to a nice firm pat, your baby will help you decide where that is

    vi.     Breast fed babies don't burp as often as bottle fed babies. So if you notice your baby doesn't burp much when mom breast feeds, it's not because your baby is all prim and proper, it's just that bottles produce more gas. More gas = more burps.

    vii.     If the baby does not burp after a few minutes, then continue feeding

    viii.     If the baby does burp, there will likely be some spittle or puke that you will need to clean off their face with the burp cloth as you lay them back into the crook of your arm

n. Repeat these steps until the baby is finished eating. Sometimes that means that they are just not hungry anymore, and sometimes you've reached the end of the bottle

13. Now that baby is fed, it's a good idea to walk around and continue patting the baby on the back to see if they have any more reflux or gas that needs to be expressed

14. Before putting the baby back down, check again if you need to change the diaper. Sometimes filling the baby up at one end, causes the other end to expel.

15. Some parents will tell you that you can change the diaper before feeding if the baby is too sleepy to eat. Other parents will tell you, not to wake you baby, when they are hungry. Every baby will be different; you will just need to make your best guess.

## Instruction 15 – Doctors, immunizations and more

1. Your newborn will see the doctor often during the first year, and not because they're sick. As a practice they need to be seen early on to make sure they are healthy once they go home and to make sure they are getting enough to eat and to deal with any issues that may come up

2. Prior to delivering you should have picked out a pediatrician or family doctor who will follow your babies care as they grow older. Below are the standard activities from each of these types of visits.

3. 2 Week visit – normally after coming home from the hospital the first "Well Baby" visit where the doctor will check the weight, height and head circumference of the baby and review the growth and development averages. Some doctors may want to repeat the newborn screen test and if not given at the hospital will administer a Hepatitis B vaccine.

4. Two Month checkup
   a. Examination of your infant's growth and development.
   b. Review of feeding and sleep schedules.

    c. Screening height, weight and head circumference.
    d. Counseling for injury prevention and diet.
    e. Immunizations: Prevnar, DTaP, HepB, Hib, IPV
5. Four Month checkup
    a. Examination of your infant's growth and development.
    b. Review of feeding and sleep schedules.
    c. Screening height, weight and head circumference.
    d. Counseling for injury prevention and diet.
    e. Immunizations: Prevnar, DTaP, Hib, IPV
6. Six Month Checkup
    a. Examination of your infant's growth and development.
    b. Review of feeding and sleep schedules.
    c. Screening height, weight and head circumference.
    d. Counseling for injury prevention, dental health, and diet.
    e. Immunizations: Prevnar, DTaP, Hib
7. Nine Month Checkup
    a. Examination of your infant's growth and development.
    b. Review of feeding and sleep schedules.
    c. Screening height, weight and head circumference.
    d. Counseling for injury prevention, dental health, and diet.
    e. Immunizations: HepB.
    f. Screening test: blood level to check for anemia, screening questionnaire for lead poisoning risk
8. Twelve Month Checkup
    a. Examination of your infant's growth and development.
    b. Review of feeding and sleep schedules.
    c. Screening height, weight and head circumference.
    d. Counseling for injury prevention, dental health, and diet.
    e. Immunizations: Prevnar, Hib, IPV, MMR, Varivax

9.  Immunization Schedule – The following chart illustrates the normal immunization schedule for your child

| Newborn | HepB #1 | | | | |
| --- | --- | --- | --- | --- | --- |
| 2 Months | DTaP#1 | Hib#1 | IPV#1 | HepB#2 | Prevnar#1 |
| 4 Months | DTaP#2 | Hib#2 | IPV#2 | Prevnar#2 | |
| 6 Months | DTaP#3 | Hib#3 | IPV#3 | HepB#3 | Prevnar#3 |
| 12 Months | Hib#4 | MMR#1 | Varicella | Prevnar#4 | |
| 15 Months | DTaP#4 | | | | |
| 2 Years | HepA | | | | |
| 4 Years | DTaP#5 | IPV#4 | MMR#2 | | |
| 12 Years | Td | | | | |

This chart is just a guide, consult your pediatrician for the immunization plan that they recommend.


**Instruction 17 – Other items of notable importance**

1.  Remember that a baby in the home should add to your life, not take away from it.  Don't forget to set up special times for you and your baby mama to get away for a night and go to the movies, dinner or just take a nap.
2.  Take turns in everything – raising a child is no longer just a woman's work.  If you believed that, you probably would never have read this book.  We have an equal responsibility in caring for, nurturing and shaping our childrens' lives.

3.  Keep healthy and strong – over the years your kids will get sick and will try to pass it on. You need to keep yourself healthy and exercise regularly to fight off these normal childhood illnesses. By doing so you will have more energy to keep up with your children.
4.  Don't make your house so quiet that a mouse skittering across the floor would sound like an elephant. If you keep your life normal with all the sounds and disturbances that go with it, babies will learn to sleep through the noise. Many people vacuum which helps lull babies to sleep.
5.  Make sure you get as much sleep as you can. If you are taking turns at night to get up and feed baby, you are going to loose 2 to 4 hours of sleep a night. Most of us need 8 hours to remain whole, but for the first several months you will only get 4 to 6 hours if you are lucky. Even then, sleep is restless as every noise the baby makes is a cause for concern. The good news is that this time period does end and you will be able to enjoy sleep again.
6.  Reconnect with your baby mama, there are few times for intimacy when competing for sleep, breast feeding, normal household chores and trying to fit in some quality time. It is imperative that you be the romantic and remember to get her flowers when the baby arrives or when she first comes home. You can get the baby a stuffed animal.
7.  Visitors will constantly interrupt your normal lifestyle during the first couple of months. Everyone wants to see the baby and the nursery and they all pick the time when you've both let yourselves go due to lack of sleep. Still well wishers will come whether you are okay with it or not. Just remember that in the first few months the baby has no immunizations and being too close to other people or to children who may be in a day care or school environment carry loads of germs. You don't want to go overboard, but perhaps not everyone needs to be in baby's face.

8.  Don't be afraid to take baby with you. Babies are a part of you now and belong in your world. Sure, they will fuss, cry, poop and embarrass you in ways you've never imagined, but in the end introducing them to social situations will help them adjust to the world.

**Instruction 18 – The final word…or words**

1.  As a father we have very little face time with our children. In fact one of the few times we can connect is as they are going to bed. This is the perfect time to read to them and its best to start at birth.
2.  Your reading material matters very little during the first month, just the sounds and pattern of your voice is enough to develop the bond of father and child
3.  There is no need to read a novel out loud unless you really want to, but just a few minutes every night, making it a routine will go miles in their long term development.
4.  I won't make any specific recommendation on what books you can buy to help your child develop as they grow, but I understand the Just For Daddy group offers a wonderful collection of book series including, _Daddy Spoke Baby_, _Toddler Talks_ and _Daddy's Girl/Boy_ designed specifically with the man in mind. Still, just about any book would do in a pinch, as long as you read to them.
5.  Children enjoy hearing rhythmic sounds and stories with rhymes and poems work well. As they get older introduce books that have more of a story so they can hear the rise and fall of your voice as they learn about emotions. And finally, they can read to you and pick up on the same techniques you used with them
6.  Children who listen to stories… read earlier, have better comprehensive skills, have better communication skills and are generally smarter… give your child a head start

7. Last and not least, this instruction section ended with 18... for no other reason than I wanted to end on a number that reflected one of my favorite games; golf. I can't wait until my kids are old enough to play a round with me... I can them teach the fine art of golf excuses (no need to elaborate.)

This image is here simply because fighter planes are cool! I am going to create a number counting book for kids with aircraft next ☺

Thank you for reading this book, I hope it was informative as well as entertaining. Being a father is not difficult, basically if you can have kids, you can be a dad. The trick is doing it well enough to transform you into a daddy.

> *Daddy – adj. A term of endearment reserved for someone who cares and tends for children, who looks out for their welfare and aids in nurturing and developing those children.*

My daughter thought it would be cute to identify the traits of a good daddy… I added some point of reference

- A daddy is patient… when she explains why she colored all over the dining room wall
- A daddy is kind… because he let her have desert, even though she colored on the wall
- A daddy is strong… you need to be to chase the monsters out from under beds
- A daddy is generous… a kind way of saying that if she sees a doll in the store and wants it, she knows I will give it to her, it's mommy's job to say no
- A daddy is clever… you need to be because they will pull every trick in the book on you
- A daddy is smart… plays on the previous, but basically not only can you see through walls, you can see through a child's tall tales
- A daddy is fair… when playing checkers or tic tac toe, sometimes you gotta let the kid win
- A daddy loves mommy… it helps tremendously when both parents are together and can contribute to the child's upbringing. Sometimes those families are broken and mommy and daddy are not together. It's much harder but still so very important to present a unified front and show the

child that they are a product of love, and love has promise and possibility

- A daddy works hard... sure, mommy does too, but the perception is that daddy is not around all the time because he works so very hard, which is probably true, but make sure you have time every day to be involved in their little lives so as they get bigger you are still a part of it.

Good luck to you new daddy... You are going to need it!

## Please pick up a copy of one of our other Daddy Survival Books or Daddy Children Books

### Daddy Survival Guide: Surviving Baby's First Year and other Post Traumatic Hormone Changes of the Mommy

Sequel to the Daddy Survival Guide, we pick up where we left off as there is far more for a new daddy to know about their growing child. In this book we discuss the phases of your childs development through the first year. No, he won't have a pitching arm yet, but he can be exposed to all things Baseball/Football...

### Daddy Survival Guide: Body Language, Sign Language...when will my 3 month old start talking - a guide to communicating with prespeech toddlers

Third in the Series, we discuss the current popular methods of communicating with babies and how to train your child to give you visual and verbal indicators for things they want or need and then build on that to formulate long term communication skills.

### Daddy Survival Guide: Walking, Talking and Creating Havoc - Understanding your Toddler

Fourth in the series of the Daddy Survival Guide, we see that our child has taken control of the house and has learned a few choice words. Unfortunately some of those you did not expect to teach them resulting in some rather embarrassing moments in church. The child or demon (your choice of identification) has also learned how to break through all the child safety devices and if they don't kill themselves, they may burn the house down. Understand how to keep your child in check, while respecting their need to grow and stretch their creative minds.

## Daddy Survival Guide: Reading, Riting & Rithmatic - Early Childhood Education

Are you seriously going to wait until your child is in kindergarten before they learn to read, write and count? Many parents do, and some because they are too busy or don't understand the importance of early at home education. My child is brilliant...yet he can't read. Your child should be well on their way to reading and basic math by age 4. School will help refine their skills, but it is up to us as parents to keep our children ahead of the learning curve by making learning fun and filling the need of their creative minds.

## If Daddy Spoke Baby – Infant Book Series

These rhythmic children's books are designed to be read by fathers to their infant children. The subject matter is manly, while put into an easy to follow rhyming pattern that newborns to toddlers enjoy hearing. Low male voice tones help encourage listening and comprehension.

## Toddler Talks – Toddler Book Series

Toddlers learn to speak, recognize and identify objects in their pre-reading stage. During this time books about objects are best to read to children pointing out common items including tools, cars, golf clubs and other items that dads find interesting and cool.

## Daddy's Boy/Daddy's Girl – Early Reader Series

Children just learning to read will find these books of interest and impact. Normal words for normal speak are used, and if a daddy did his job with the first two series, the early reader will not only learn how to read but will also understand more complex words.

Please visit www.daddysurvivalguide.com to order your books directly! Also visit www.justfordaddy.com for all your daddy needs.

Thank You,


Alex Willis
Ultimate Man/ Ultimate Dad